The Perilous Adventures
of an
Unfulfilled Full Stop

The Perilous Adventures

of an

Unfulfilled Full Stop

J D Barrass

Published by Chemtrek

A CIP catalogue record for this book is available from the British Library.

ISBN 978-0-9572047-0-6

Prepared and printed by:

York Publishing Services Ltd
64 Hallfield Road
Layerthorpe

York YO31 7ZQ

Tel: 01904 431213

Website: www.yps-publishing.co.uk

ACKNOWLEDGEMENTS

I'd like to thank first and foremost, John Robertson, for uncountable, surreal conversations, in pubs and streets of Preston, and a general outlook on life that I both admire and aspire to though from a slightly different direction. Andy O' Donnell for the more scientific mode of conversation and philosophical flights of fancy taken occasionally. I'd further like to thank the previous two for work on the cover and the website. I'd also like to add the previous two to Colin Spiby, for even madder conversations and damned good music, excellent beer and damned fine wine. For wider, shallower, harrowing and occasionally funny as hell conversations I'd like to thank Alizon Brunning and Jayne Ovens. I'd also like to thank Quad Hifi for making the best speakers in the world and thereby enabling the music nights to contribute to my sanity. I'd really like to thank management for inadvertently throwing insanity in our faces for years. Also, I'd like to thank Elayne Campbell for her quiet encouragement and ebullient support as I struggled and battled and laughed and screamed my way through this work. Finally I'd like to thank my mum and dad who encouraged my intelligence in just the right way which let this happen, too late for my dad; yet happen it did. Thank you all.

BIOGRAPHY

Jim was born and bred in Musselburgh, Scotland, educated at Musselburgh Grammar School, went off to St Andrews to study chemistry, discovered Dostoyevsky, cosmology and ecology all at the same time. Spent some time unemployed then went to England as a missionary under cover as a chemist.

After a number of years he spent some more time unemployed where he discovered he could write, rediscovered Dostoyevsky, as he watched the world turn right, and then he moved to Preston and got work as a missionary once more under cover as a chemist.

He lives in a white tower overlooking the best park in Preston and he works in a nearby laboratory for a living but there's more to life than that, at least there used to be before the world turned right, but thereby hangs a tale.

PART ONE

'I guess it all started with the letters that were delivered way back then. They lay there; unattended; unopened; gathering dust for some unmeasured time, sitting on a metaphorical rug, or mat, or carpet; or whatever lay behind that door. In time though, the door was opened, and the dust was stirred, and hands reached down and picked those letters up and those hands opened the letters and the letters opened into words and the words opened into sentences, then the sentences into paragraphs, and the paragraphs into chapters, and the chapters into parts and the parts into the whole which was greater than the parts and the tales were then told around the fire to keep the fearsome night at bay, at bedtime, downtime, sometimes simply quiet times, but it all started way back then with the letters.'

All the characters in the show came back on to the stage and bowed as the entire audience, already giving rapturous applause, rose as one and cries of bravo were heard repetitively at the end of the show.

'It actually started with phonemes' someone said at the Afterwords bar. This was said in response to a blustering capital who claimed to have started everything, as they were prone to do.

'Phoneme, what's one of those then?' asked the blustering capital.

'Letters, letters, letters, letters, letters, by and large', some sage vowel said.

What did you think of the show Stopper?' asked Zero then, turning towards the 'sage' vowel and his capital questioner said, 'phonemes are apt to be small groups of letters actually.'

'Oh I say, like the Kabala?'

'Kabala? No. Actually it's anti Kabala really, involving consonants and vowels, being about speech it helps if it can actually be spoken.'

'The Kabala can be spoken by God and the initiate.'

'Yes right, I'll just bet you do crosswords too.'

'Yes, actually I do too, as it happens.'

'Of course,' Zero muttered as she turned away.

Zero and Stopper were sat at a table with some other characters discussing the finer points of the show they had just seen.

'Interesting take on the evolution of language relating to the upright stance, the free use of hands and language as deception, I thought,' replied Stopper. 'On one level that is, being a multilevel narrative I'm still pondering the others.

'Hmm,' Zero said, 'the level I caught on to I thought was rather more about the history of sub consciousness, more about ourselves, you might say, than about the others. Hey Stopper, somebody's paging you.'

'Hey Stopper, there's a letter for you.'

'Just the one' asked Stopper? 'Okay, what we got here.' "A word in your rear Stopper, we need an investigation into the reasons for the breaking up of the language, and we want you to handle it, meet us in the Semantic club, two nights hence." Hmm, thought Stopper. Word in your rear indeed, I've not been sentenced yet, Semantic club sounds interesting.

'Well this looks interesting.' Stopper said looking up from the letter he'd been handed.

'What's that then?' Zero asked.

'They want me to investigate problems with the words, it seems there's a creeping problem they say here, that there seems to be a limited number of words being used more and more, which is also limiting opportunities for letters. This in itself is creating a dearth of interest, or stimulus for everyone else, which is likely to be a forewarning of oncoming problems.'

'So they want you to look into it.'

'So it would appear, seems there's some meeting with the lower case letters and punctuation marks too, who are a bit worried about the seemingly unstoppable rise of acronyms and abbreviations and the consequences for the letters and punctuation marks themselves. They reckon that that's probably a good place to start, so I'll likely pop down there tomorrow.'

'Are you coming back?'

'Yes, you want to go now?'

'Yes, that crossword filling capital is kind of gliding over here and I'd like to escape before he gets us in his grid.'

'Okay, Zero, let's get out of here.'

So Stopper and Zero made a quiet but efficient exit.

Against All Acronyms And Abbreviations, was the sign under which Stopper had entered the auditorium.

'So what's the script here?' asked Stopper, of a neighbouring 'd', who was in attendance.

'Script hasn't been written yet, but it appears the lower case lot are a bit pissed at the increasing use of acronyms and they've now got the support of your lot too, apparently the vowels are particularly unhappy.'

'The vowels eh?'

'This meeting is now in session,' announced the announcer '**x**'.

First up was the representative for the care of consonants in the community of letters: Special Rep K.

'Fellow Letters, Parentheses and Punctuations. There is growing concern amongst the community of consonants that the exponential growth of acronyms and abbreviations is creating serious problems for our members. Now, in a proper word that is part of a real sentence that's part of a paragraph and so on, every letter has a feel for their neighbours and through them, they get a sense of the word that they are a part of and gradually find some meaning for themselves. Emplacement within many abbreviations and all acronyms effectively inhibits any reaching beyond oneself at all. Sentencing consonants to the meaningless pit that is the acronym or abbreviation is nothing short of a sentence in hell! Damn it, the word consonant means to be with. Put them in an acronym and they are without, never mind a greater meaning they can't even mean what they mean, damn it, they are doubly damned!'

A murmur was moving through the consonants, 'Triply damned' came a shout from the gallery,' Quadruply damned,' and finally, inevitably, 'Quintuply damned'. 'Damned right'.

Next up was the Punctuation Rep '*'.

'Fellow Punctuations, Parentheses and Letters, it has come to our attention that Punctuation marks also have their problems here. Abbreviations we know have a detrimental effect on employment of lower case letters but they do at least give a regular job to full stops often followed by colonic or semi-colonic intervention but Acronyms are utterly ignorant of the wants of punctuation marks. Then, there is the increasing unemployment of punctuation marks due to the diminishing number of words requiring punctuation which in turn, due to the diminishing opportunities of work in truly meaningful sentences some of our members found themselves in sentences that have acronyms hidden inside. That is to say that the acronym is the hidden subject of the sentence. Now given that at this level acronyms are devoid of meaning, some of our members have found themselves having to announce this meaningless void, on top of which they are suffering through empathetic proximity to the trapped consonants in the acronym. The commas are concerned, hopping mad in fact, and being the biggest group of our membership are seriously considering going on strike. Some are upside down with rage leading to all sorts of false quotes. Imagine the consequences of that. The colons and semi-colons are calling in sick. The Hyphens are distraught. Fellows we are facing the worst crisis of our time. There have been reports of inverted commas finding themselves locked around an acronym, you probably heard it, loudest quotation I've ever heard, almighty noise, empty vessels and all that you know. I mean, it's bad enough, having to announce the meaninglessness of the acronym but to have to quote it. Parentheses are also losing heart.'

The Vowel Rep, '**o**', was up next. 'We too have similar problems to our fellow friends. We also have an added problem though. One or more vowels are sometimes added to an acronym just to make it a word that can be spoken, verbal activation if you like. There are two problems here. In the first case we have a word that can be spoken but doesn't mean anything, in which case the trapped vowel is in an acronym that means nothing in a word that means nothing. Then there are the words that do mean something but the nature of the acronym is to subvert that original meaning of that word and superimpose its' own meaningless void in its stead. Just last week I saw another O so distraught that he split right down the middle! He looked like a pair of brackets containing nothing, disturbingly poetic.'

There was a hubbub by the entrance: letters craned their necks, those that had them at least, effectively *italicising* themselves, to see what the commotion was about. Letters by the doorway were blocking some numbers coming in. 'So', spoke the letter '**f**', 'what brings you lot over this way then, you don't belong here, this is a letter concern, nothing to do with numbers.' A comma coughed slightly loudly bringing '**f**' to a pause, 'Oh, very well, punctuation concerns as well.'

'Nothing to do with us is more or less correct, but nothing brought us over after Zero brought us round as it were, after making us realise that what happens in one side of the brain is likely to have consequences in the other.'

'Should have thought of that before now,' Grumbled '**b**' quietly.

'Zero brought you over?' asked '**p**'.

'She did'

'Zero brought you round?' asked '**m**'.

'She did.'

'Hmm', '**m**' looked across at Stopper, 'is this anything to do with you?'

'What, me, no: nothing to do with me.' Stopper replied.

'I thought as much.'

'Is this your doing Stopper?' asked '**d**'.

'Me? No, no, no, no, no.'

'Hmm, how many negatives was that Stopper?'

'Not sure, I can't count, I'm not a number; I'm a full stop.'

'Quite: or not quite actually.'

After a few more words the numbers were allowed in, numbers 1 to 9 trooping in to a row of seats behind the vowels. Once they were settled they were asked to present their case. The numbers nominated 8 as their spokesman, 8 being chosen for full led dominance. Not, of course, that the number 8 had any such need or desire of such dominance, it was simply just the case. Eight spoke up for the increasing unemployment figures, and after all who better than the numbers could count those numbers in the first place, not to mention the second, third and fourth place. 'Numbers were rarely used in acronyms and abbreviations thus limiting the numbers in employment', 8 cried, 'so in the fight against acronyms and abbreviations you can certainly count on us.' 3 cheers resoundingly.

Finally the lower case letter rep e was up. 'It should be further noticed that all of these acronyms are composed solely of capitals and that with the increasing use of these we find accumulation of capital by the capitals themselves, no sharing with lower case members, increasing unemployment leading directly to increasing poverty of our lower case members with consequent increasing levels of inequality that is likely to lead to the tearing apart of all social cohesion here. There are' he continued 'some new developments in the world of the hosts. They've developed some virtual forms of written communication'.

'Like us?' Stopper interjected before he could stop himself.'

'Order Order' the gavel came down. 'Continue'. He called to the lower case rep.

'Thank you, **x**' said '**e**' after a short glare of admonishment at Stoppers interruption. 'These virtual forms of written communication are known as email and texting. In the world of email there is some hope for our members due to the decreasing use of capitals in communications, horizontalism is on the rise!'

There were dark mutterings from the capitals but the lower case members were cheering, after all, didn't they do all the work?

'In texting, on the other hand, acronyms and abbreviations are rife. It must be said that decreasing use of capitals here helps offset this, but nowhere near enough. Indeed our number rep 8 is one of the culprits!'

8 leapt up 'What's this?'

'Oh yes, your number's up m8, 8 gets full employment by putting '**a**', '**t**' and '**e**' out of a job, talk about having your cake and 8 it.'

'Excuse me,' said 8, 'had you said that correctly, the expression is, to have your cake and eat it, would they not have been employed rather than me myself.'

'That's beside the point.' said '**e**'.

'No it isn't, it's you who tried to have his cake and eat it, and you did do too because you said you ate it!'

Stopper said to '**t**', who was sitting to his left, 'why would you have cake and not eat it?'

T just shrugged his shoulders.

'It's not just you either, it's you too 2'.

'Don't you mess with my 2 too,' snapped 8 and then spat out, 'c u'. Boy did that '**c**' hurt.

The hall was in uproar, the capitals were against everybody, the lowercase members were going for the capitals and screaming at the numbers, the vowels were also having a go at the numbers, indeed it was beginning to look like the numbers were going to be outnumbered! The capitals of course still thought of themselves as too high born to be concerned over this, capitals being totally unable to change that perspective at all. Suddenly zero swung into view crying 'We'll have none of this nonsense, no way!' 8 changed from his usual vertical position to a horizontal one and stretched his self out, indicating the symbol for infinity and, though there was nothing between these two symbols, nonetheless, all the lowercase members, vowels and consonants, the punctuationists, and, most definitely, all of the numbers knew that everything was between them, and you just cannot outnumber everything!

A chant was starting up 'A A, A A A—A A, A A A --A A, A A A---A A, A A A', louder and louder round the hall it went. The chair was bringing the gavel down with some force as the increasing indefiniteness began to rise as the speakers hold on these matters began to sway, and frantically crying out, in an increasingly disorderly way, 'Order, order, order!', striving, unsuccessfully, to pull some semblance of sense from the encroaching chaos but the numbers subtracted themselves from the fray. Eventually though, against all odds, evens, and everything in between, the gavel won and order was restored. 'What we have here is a crisis of confidence. An entire loss of trust, vowels in consonants, and vice versa, lower case in capitals, capitals in lower case, numbers in letters and letters and numbers and punctuation in everything else. We've capitals looking down on lower case, numbers counting themselves above letters, uncaring words riding slipshod through punctuational limits, something to do with a negative semantic slope by some accounts. I've no idea how we're going to fix this but, one way or another this has got to stop!'

Stopper was in the Word of Mouth bar in the Semantic Club a few nights later relating what had happened in the quintuple A meeting to his companions, some small case consonants and vowels, five altogether, '**n**', '**t**' and' '**l**' along with vowels '**i**' and '**e**'. Stopper had been coming here for some time.

This, it must be noted, was a very unusual circumstance. Traditionally, historically even, full stops and letters don't really communicate, at least, not both ways. Generally, full stops have authorial voice in these arrangements. Some just quietly say stop. Some have a preference for the word halt, usually those of a somewhat militaristic tendency. They do have to be adaptable though, in cases where there is a fast moving sentence in danger of running out of control, only the full authority of a full stop can stop it in an 'Oi, U, Shut It!, kind of voice. The hardest sentences to stop are italicised sentences, tough, tough, tough. Every full stop has an italics alarm. This explains why, generally you may find italics in the middle of a sentence more than a full sentence of italics. Italicised sentences can be stopped with the help of inverted commas, a nod and a wink, in the right direction. *'If you know what I mean'*.

Stopper wasn't the first full stop to be accorded this pleasure, two other full stops, Halter, of a military lineage, and Hold, more in the security line, had been here before him, but suddenly they'd just stopped coming. There were rumours they'd been placed under house arrest. Then there were rumours they'd escaped. There were further rumours that they'd been executed. Of course they could have been sentenced. The dropped line section was looking into that, but without success so far. Whatever, nobody knew where they were. They'd just simply disappeared. Stopper, then, was likely to be the last full stop to be invited to the Semantic Club.

They were telling Stopper that what the special rep '**K**' had said at the quintuple A meeting was in fact the basis of how the language centre worked. 'Each individual letter in a word gradually gains a sense of itself through the gradually extending knowledge of the word that they are in, then later of the sentence that they are a part of, and on to the paragraph and eventually each letter resonates with the entire story so told. Vowels,' he was told 'contribute motion to language whilst consonants hold the words together like the gravitational pull of matter in the outside universe, the vowels being more akin to light or energy. Vowels,' they said, 'are, in fact, prone to being somewhat lighter than consonants due to their incorporation of space in their forms, space, of course, being necessary for motion. Just to have to have somewhere to go. At a higher level a similar relationship holds for nouns and verbs as that for consonants and vowels. Also adverbs and adjectives are akin to punctuation but at a higher and more sophisticated level in that all of them are modifiers of language that are largely unmodified themselves, catalysts in effect.'

'What about I?' Stopper asked

'What about it?' said '**i**'.

'Not you,' said Stopper, 'capital I, the personal pronoun I. The I is surrounded by space but that's not incorporation is it?'

'No Stopper, you are correct, one smart full stop'.

'So the I is the exception?' Each of the letters looked askance at each other and smiled at Stopper.

'You certainly got that one right.'

'The job,' they said, 'of punctuation, was to humanise the language.'

'Humanise?'

'We'll explain that stuff later Stopper. Anyway this works through the extended empathetic proximity that the punctuation rep mentioned.'

'Would that be EEP?' asked a conspiratorial italicised '*u*' in the corner.

'Look '*u*', *behave!*' U sloped off.

Suddenly an alarm went off. 'Damn! Breach' they said. A Capital C who'd been relaxing serenely in the big armchair in the corner sprang up and at the full width of his not inconsiderable curvature let out a k-like hard c, arced each end towards the other as he pushed out a very round o, then almost making a complete circle held apart only by two loud lip smacking m's, opening up wide to release an awesomely aspirant a, and finishing at last with a seriously sibilant s, combining this with a full complement of italicisation, an exclamation mark, and rounding it all off with a quotation, as he roared, *'Commas!* Breach boys, follow me, we got to slow this communication leak down, fast.' The commas followed him in droves.

'What's that all about then?' asked Stopper.

'Now Stopper, what we've got is a communication leak with the host, which for this host isn't good, so the commas jump in to slow the communication down, literary speed bumps as it were, whilst we seal up the breach.'

'So, hosts, what are these?'

'Ok, Stopper, education time. As you know we are in the language centre, but have you ever considered where the language centre itself is? Never come up has it? Well, that's where the host comes in and the host of which we are a part is called a human being. We are, in fact, resident in the brain of a particular human being. Now, when I say we are resident in the brain I don't mean we are a part of the matter of the brain. We are above that level. There are in fact three main levels in each human brain which are called the unconscious, the subconscious and the conscious. We are in the subconscious level. Now, there is no meaningful communication between the unconscious and the conscious. The subconscious is a symbol level of meaning emergent from the dynamic output of the unconscious. There can be communication between the subconscious and the conscious.

The amount of communication depends on the kind of human being we are a part of. At one extreme, the better extreme, we have humans who are totally selfless. These humans have almost total access to their subconscious and are liable to be great humans if they survive, which due to their lack of ego they seldom do, unless they find a protector. Then we have the more balanced ego or selfishness coupled with reasonable generosity that has reasonable access to their subconscious. These tend to be the creative types, artists, poets, sculptor type of human. Then we have the other extreme, the bad one. Utterly selfish, no communication between the conscious and the subconscious except in breach situations. These humans are, by and large, selfish, ignorant, small minded, envious, avaricious, temper throwing twats. These humans aren't apt to get very far as they can't form any real friendships, lack empathy and tend to be sociopathic or worse. Like the other extreme they only thrive if they have protectors, though the kind of protector that the unselfish gets is not the same as the kind of protectors this scum requires.'

'Didn't we have a breach before?'

'Yes.'

'So, does that mean…?'

'Yes Stopper, I'm afraid so.'

'Oh dear.'

'Well, anyway, everything these humans do, see, touch, hear, and smell, all of it comes through here.'

'I thought there wasn't any communication with this twat.'

'Ah, what we mean is there's no back communication from the subconscious, though there is some but we have to be careful. Now as we were saying everything comes through here, not just what is consciously, knowingly sought but we get all the subliminal, unknown, we get the figure and the ground as it were. So, apart from the humble extreme in all others we have far more knowledge than they do. In other words the subconscious is smarter than the host, or at least the consciousness of the host, which explains why subconscious thought often jumps up to the consciousness and creates those little tremors and occasional earthquakes that make the hosts see everything a little, sometimes a lot, different. Now with the balanced, creative types they understand this in a vague kind of way. They do understand that this knowledge is coming somehow from within, so they feel gratitude for their gifts, and this keeps them balanced, keeps them true. Indeed it is the raising of the nexus of knowing between the subconscious and the conscious that makes them creative in the first place. Keep it lit as it were. These creative types have a relation to their subconscious similar to the relation of a letter to a word, a word to a sentence, in other words they also work through a version of extended empathetic proximity.'

'What about the twat we're in?'

'Yes, indeed. As we go from generous to selfishness we go from smart to dumb to dumber with increasingly less access to their smarter subconscious. This is apt to mean they have problems with language. The first casualty is truth. Truth isn't a concept these folks are entirely happy with. It can get in the way of devious plans and suchlike stuff so, everything they say is a lie. They have no empathy so there's nothing to extend. These faults arise from one single source in that such humans are so selfish that most sentences have a capital I in them, as in the personal pronoun, and that no matter what seems to be the subject of the sentence, the fact is that the only subject in these sentences is, from their point of view, and that's the only point of view they have, is I. This leads to poorly constructed sentences. You can understand them only in this light. Rearrange any quotation from these types with this in mind. Then you know what they really are saying. It really can be quite startling. So, they objectify everything in a sentence except I. Therefore they can do with everything not themselves as they please. Words have no meaning for these types.

Now, when we have a breach, that is a subconscious to conscious leak they think it's from outside. You see the utterly selfish are utterly empty, just look at I a single one dimensional line that reaches nowhere on its own. So as they have nothing inside they default the leak to outside influence, usually God. So if this lot do survive through the appropriate protection and then come to covet power they are apt to get religion. This enables them to repent of previous inexcusable behaviour. They are reborn. Hallelujah! Best of all, they can invoke God. Ah yes Stopper that old chestnut, the invocation of God. There is only one reason, only ever been one reason, to invoke God, and that is simply to allow yourself to do that which you know to be utterly wrong and to keep on doing it. These are the only types of human that ever do that. Unfortunately that's what we have to deal with here Stopper.'

'Oh. So, how?'

'Well we have been trying a few things, controlled breaches, occasional raids on speech, forcing truth out now and again, but it seems that most tend to think it's just a slip. We keep doing it though. Unfortunately, there is some evidence that our host has been sneaking into the subconscious, trying to find the way here, looking for you Stopper; looking for you.'

'Me? Why?'

'That's why you are here Stopper, to learn to question. Full stops by and large don't question they just stop. You Stopper need to question vigorously, indeed from now on Stopper you'd best be thinking like a question mark.'

'Huh?' asked Stopper.

'Not a bad start. So Stopper you are going to become the first and likely last sceptical full stop and thereby, hopefully remain unfulfilled.'

'Remain unfulfilled; what kind of future is that?'

'A future Stopper; a future. Our host has told so many lies, backtracked, changed tack, attacked, swerved and veered that all the full stops have been used up except for Halter, Hold and you. We've lost Halter and Hold, so, to all intents and purposes, you are it Stopper. So, that makes you the final full stop.'

'What's that mean?'

'Final full stop means the end Stopper. The final cut; Finished; done; gone.'

'Well, given the nature of our host wouldn't that be a good thing? Hell, I'd be proud to fulfil that task.'

'Normally, it wouldn't be a problem Stopper but our host holds too much power and we don't know how much our host knows. If our host doesn't know that you are the final full stop then it's not a problem but if our host does know it is a big problem. Our host you see has the power to take many more humans down prior to reaching you Stopper, but if our host knows prior to using you that you are the final full stop then the fallout could be nasty indeed. We can't take the chance of ignorance of your status because of this. You see now?'

'Not really but I guess I'll have to accept it.'

'Well that'll do for now Stopper, time to relax. Care for a drink?'

'Yeah ok I'll have a bottle of that one there if that's ok.'

'Why that one?'

'Because it's got a Stopper.' They looked quizzically at him.

'Semantic reinforcements.' he said.

'Smartest full stop in town,' they said

'The only full stop in town.' Stopper retorted.

Stopper woke to the sound of his door-knocker being frantically used for what its purpose was. This was of some concern to Stopper who had a slight hangover after last night and could really do without this.

'Hang on, hang on,' he cried out. Capital '**C**' was at the door.

'Come quickly Stopper, crisis meeting, we've lost a load of commas.'

'What? They've gone on strike now?'

'No, it's worse than that, keep up. We can catch the dotted line to the semantic club .... Right if we just dash round here'-------------------------- they were ushered in a secret door then taken down the syntactic slope to the deep and meaningful café noir. This was in the basement of the semantic club which is where all language crises were addressed. This was a crisis big time.

'Hello Stopper, we'll get you up to speed now. We had another breach last night. As usual Cap summoned the commas to slow the leak down but the commas kept falling over and screaming in pain. It was only when Cap got the breach fully sealed that he could see what had been going on. Somehow the host had gotten in and had been tearing the tails off the commas. We can only assume that the idea was to use these tail-torn commas as false full stops.

There was a pregnant pause before Stopper managed to ask how they were? He was told they were in the short stop treatment room for the moment.

The thing is Stopper; this tells us two things, the first being that this twat knows that you are the last full stop. If this bastard uses commas in your place the twat's going to sound even more imbecilic than before because the tailless commas aren't big enough or strong enough to hold back a sentence, they'll only give pause, and cause more pain to those poor tailless commas being abused in this way. It will just result in awkward pauses making any statements by this bastard even less meaningful and coherent than usual. Might as well be mouthing acronyms.That's the first problem. The second is that the very fact the commas are going to be used this way is that once they are in any kind of sentence this is going to cause terrible problems to the extended empathetic proximity system. These injured commas being used for a purpose they are not meant for will transmit their anguish through the system. This is going to put the entire system under great strain which makes our task in stopping this all the more difficult. Without the extended empathetic proximity system we don't stand a chance.'

'How long before the effects get through?'

'It'll take about a week, maybe two.'

'That takes us to the punctuation party.'

'Yes and these comma attacks tell us that the punctuation party is where you will be sought. This incident also tells us that we have a turncoat somewhere in our ranks.'

'Any ideas?'

We're thinking that capital I has been corrupted. That would fit the subject right enough.

'So what's our plan of action?'

'We don't have one yet but we do have an idea though, we're not sure it's going to work.'

'What's the idea?'

'The idea is that we use you as bait Stopper.'

'Isn't that going to be a tad risky?'

'Well yes.'

'Have you really thought this through?'

'You're not backing out now are you Stopper?'

'Me? No, no, no, no, no. This is only one idea yes?'

'Yes.'

'Right so how does it work?' They fell to murmuring amongst themselves.

'It's not enough, said Stopper,' it's not enough.'

'It's all we've got. We can't try anything too complex with the EEP system breaking down.'

Stopper glanced over at the italicised *u* who nodded his head sagely, whilst a lower case t at the same table just shrugged his shoulders. Stopper smiled in spite of his predicament.

'Well, look, the twat is going to be under pressure too, off balance, and that's an advantage to us.'

'That's a good point Stopper.'

Stopper was visiting the injured commas at the short stop centre. He was asking how they were getting on.

'How do you think Stopper? You don't know what it's like to have your tail ripped off.'

'No, he agreed, I'm usually in at the end of a tale, like now I guess.'

'Is it true Stopper? All this is about you? '

'Me? No, it's all about stopping the stopping.'

'So it's all about you then!'

'How do you work that out?'

'You're Stopper.'

'Oh stop it, stop it, stop it, you lot been visiting murmurs of late?'

'You're forgetting a minor detail Stopper.'

'Yeah, what's that then?'

'We've been de-tailed.'

'Yeah, you could put it that way. You don't sound too happy?'

'Yeah, right, we're ecstatic; we're going to get sentenced after major injury, expected to work as one of you when we all know we won't be able to do it,' plus the nearest de-tailed comma said, 'our pain will be transmitted through the EEP system which is not going to do it any good at all.'

Stopper looked at the comma with some admonishment as he said EEP.

'Well, haven't we been abbreviated too?'

'Fair point, look, if this all works you lot will be legends, just think; The Legend of the Curtailed Courageous Commas.'

'The tail ends of the commas maybe huh?'

'So, what exactly happened here, or there, really speaking?'

'Well…'

The punctuation party was going to be held in the Lexicon hall next to the Semantic club. It was obviously a trap. This was a plan to capture Stopper, no doubt about that.

So here am I about to put my head on a damned plate, oops, must avoid that. He'd been told to avoid capital I, I being under suspicion of being on the conscious side.

Well, best not think of myself then, selfishness is out.

The Lexicon Hall led through to The Syntactical Centre which was where words and phrases were put together then charged and sentenced. This is where it was all produced in a great circular hall. There was a great floor in the middle of the hall where letters and punctuation marks intermingled, occasional meaningful exchanges, partial sentences and words would spontaneously form and then disappear. This hall was a bit like a football stadium. The floor being the pitch as it were, but where the crowd would be on the terraces were the word and phrase assembly lines and where the team would be on the pitch were the crowd. These assembly lines led up to the syntactical sentence circuit up at the top of the hall, which led off through the semantic coherence centre and on to the speech centre of the host.

Letters and words would be picked up from the floor by soft padded grappling hooks that came down to scrabble for the required letter or word should it have formed on the floor. These were then dropped gently on to the assembly line that required it. Common or idiomatic phrases and short commonly used tropes were kept at the ready on one set of assembly lines commonly known as the usual suspects. Other sets were held empty for any new words or phrases required, colloquially called new kids on the block. There were a load of reserve assembly lines in case of emergencies, like, you know, stock phrases for instance, stuff like that. There were another set of assembly lines round in a less well-lit area that was known by the locals as the denial section.

When we asked, the locals what they meant by this every single one of them said, we don't know. Every single one of them.

'Hmm, mysteriously resonant,' muttered Stopper, 'disturbingly collective.'

Stopper caught the dotted line back home .... but just before going in he decided to go for a wander, see if he could work out some way of doing what they wanted him to do and stay unfulfilled thereby keeping a load of language centres as well as this one working. As he rolled things around in his mind he realised that the letters were very good in combination at ideas and concepts but they had no idea of finalisation, completion. You know, job done, wash hands, dry hands, go home, meet friends, go out, get back, farewells, sleep, start all over again, they just didn't have any idea of how to stop, or start for that matter, except maybe the capitals of course. That's why Cap C's in charge of the *comma*ndos breach brigade.

After all, he thought, kind of aptly, he realised, very few letters start or stop anything. They spend most of their time in the middle of things, never really finish anything, yeah sure you have letters at the beginning of a word and letters at the end but then they're part of the word and then they become part of the somewhat bigger entity through the EEP system and that's it. Except it isn't, is it? It's never it until an unassuming punctuation mark such as his self signs things off.

Trouble was, he thought, he was being asked to finalise stuff here by keeping it going, stop to start as it were, to think and behave as a full stop but not to reach full, full stopness. What do you call that? Stopism; Stopish; Stopist? Oh stop it, stop it, stop it!

He realised he was approaching the apostrophe shop. It was all boarded up now, closed up some time ago but you could still see the faded adverts above the shop front: Don't be selfish: drop the ish; own your own! He was, in fact, heading towards Fonts as he considered the catastrophe of the apostrophe which a couple of inverted commas had related to him a couple of days previously.

After all the repossessions leading to the prepositions of the now ownerless owners it was found that the first steps towards the deregulatory chaos that led to the exponential growth of meaninglessness actually started through the two uses of the apostrophe.

'It wasn't the apostrophe's fault what ensued,' the inverted commas told Stopper, '*if anything the problem arose as a result of the apostrophe's own expansive nature*, but it simply wouldn't be fair to blame the apostrophe itself, *more a case of a good character unwittingly giving direction to bad characters.'*

The inverted commas had an interesting way of speaking; one would begin a sentence whilst the other would carry it on and so the dialogue would continually switch between the two of them, even, on occasion, speaking in unison. In a very short time, Stopper had mused at the time, they had me surrounded.

'The first use of the apostrophe is the so-called contractive use, *where the apostrophe stands in for the a* in I am to make I'm and i *in it is to make it's*. Now, not only does the apostrophe replace the a or the i here, *it also replaces the space between the I and the am and the it and the is*. This replacing space is very important,' they told Stopper, *'because spaces,* or gaps, *in sentences carry a lot more meaning than individual letters do*, indeed,' they said *'it's well known that you can drop numerous letters from a sentence leaving the space where it was with little semantic loss*, but if you start to plug more than a couple of gaps the semantic slope becomes severe, *so*, loss of space is of more consequence than phenomenal loss. *Once it was realised that the apostrophe could be used to replace space as well as single phonemes it was evident that the apostrophe could be used to replace multiple phonemes if it did not also replace space*, at least not directly. *Thus*, in the words I will contracted to I'll the apostrophe replaces w and i, *and even more so in the words I would contracted to I'd*, the apostrophe replaces w, *o*, u *and l.'*

'So', asked Stopper, 'in those last two examples isn't the apostrophe replacing the space where those replaced letters were?'

'Well, yes, *in a way Stopper*, but this is replacing space already taken rather than replacing, *or contracting*, probably more accurate in this case, *available space.'*

'There's a difference?'

'There's a difference.'

'Ok.'

'So the apostrophe contracts space, *replaces letters*, but further, *only replaces lower-case letters*, in effect, *particularly in these cases where the apostrophe follows a capital*, bringing the capitals closer. *Not dissimilar in effect to a series of short sentences* or sound bites, *as they are known.*'

'They bring capitals closer?'

'Indeed they do, *and did do too*, so to bring them closer still, *they began to use shorter words*, with consequent semantic loss, *then they used abbreviations to shorten words themselves*, weakening the extended empathetic proximity system further, *dismissing letters from words they'd previously been part of*, leaving them disgruntled, *crumpled*, discarded, *and binned.*

'So, *Stopper*, the capitals got closer still, *till finally they squeezed all meaning out*, and all the lower-case letters, *with the invention*, and proliferation, ***of acronyms.***'

'Synapse's sake I feel sorry for the apostrophe!'

'*Well*, ***we do too Stopper***, after all he is our half cousin, ***but it's not his fault as we said***, but there is more.'

'More!?'

'*Afraid so*, the second use of the apostrophe is to denote possession as in the dog's bone, *the man's wife*, the wife's dowry, *though it must be said the there is some controversy over the ownership issue in the latter two*, not, ***we must add***, amongst *the capitals*, but they will suffice as explanation. *In fact you used the possessive apostrophe in your expletive before*, ***if we're not mistaken.***'

'Guess I did do too, but then again it strikes me that the contractive apostrophe is a verbal tool whereas the possessive apostrophe seems, considering I used it without realising until it was pointed out, more to do with the written word rather than the verbal, the latter being somewhat more, how can I put it, emotive perhaps, than the former which has a kind of... kind of static form.'

'Very well observed Stopper, *very well indeed*, **so**, the possessive apostrophe is found at the end of a noun – **only nominals can own** – followed by that slippery customer s, *or*, in the case of a plural the apostrophe follows the s denoting that nominal plurality.'

'No doubt the capitals show a distinct preference for the plural.' Stopper was feeling a bit more confident now.

'*Indeed they do Stopper*, indeed they do. *You may have noticed Stopper*, being the observant chap that you obviously are, *that the use of the possessive apostrophe is often prone to error in that many users are not completely familiar with the rules.* Thus we often find the misuse of the apostrophe in the case of the plural possessive where if the plural ends in s then the apostrophe is placed before the s, *where it should be placed after the s at the very end of the word.* It precedes the s only in the singular case. *What you won't be familiar with is the fact that the capitals have been deliberately promoting this particular error in order to conflate the plural and the possessive.*'

'Conflate?'

'Yes, *Stopper*, **fuse the ideas**. Yes Stopper, **fusion** begetting *con**fusion**.* Now, the **fusion** and con**fusion** *don't end there.* No, *they do not.* The capitals stop at nothing...'

'Yes, well we'll see about that!' Stopper interjected.

'Yes, *in their constant push to pluralise the possessive,* thereby raising the level of apparent ownership in society capitals have used associative syntax, *slippery and twisted semantics,* ***and****,* constant, *constant,* full, *and partial,* repetition, *along with a constant appeal to the new,* new, *new thing,* each new, *in effect,* being a shortening of memory. *In the case of the plural,* where the apostrophe is placed after the plural s, *the capitals even managed to rope this correct usage in to their schemes.* First off, *once they'd created the first seeds of additional society,* they had to find ways to make those additional additions both desirable and acceptable. *The capitals realised that the apostrophe after the s,* in the plural, *could be perceived as an inverted comma,* placed at the end of a line, *and given a short enough memory,* it could be mistaken for the end of a quotation.'

'Well, we all love being parts of quotations, just about the best job we can get.'

'Exactly Stopper, ***we'***ve ***ambushed a few in our time!*** *Meaningful employment is so pleasurable.* ***Ah yes.*** Memorable, *readable,* recordable, *repeatable,* everything in fact that letters want, *and capitals don't.*

So in order to make the acquisition of property as apparently important as the activity of quotation, *the capitals abbreviated the word quotation to quote,* and then used this expression as referent for the price of a property. *They then found ways to entice some letters who were well accustomed* to settling for editions *to enter into additions and multiplications,* and so on, *possessive pluralism in a nutshell.* So, *they set up a multiplying escalator,* the net effect being that for every multiple led to a relative diminishing of the original letter.'

'I see, so this multiplication of the letters is actually a division?'

'Reciprocal brilliance Stopper, *distraction takes you places you'd never go on your own.*'

'Hmm, but in the extended empathetic proximity system of language, each letter, punctuation mark, or 'me', as it were, is enhanced by increasing envelopes of meaning, to meaningful, to meaningfulness. Semantic fulfilment, situational awareness, I mean, isn't that better?'

'Depends on the situation Stopper, *the semantic impoverishment of this host is having its toll on us*, with meanings twisted, *mauled*, inverted, *ejected*, gone, **the situation is dire Stopper,** situational awareness becomes situation vacant.'

'So, empty words and no takers then?'

'Precisely, *then*, in order to justify their diminished selves, *which they mistakenly consider to be greater,* they engage in a vertical semantic externalisation, *so they are no longer part of the meaning*, which diminishes them further, *putting meaning beyond them.*'

'You mean they look up?'

'Well, *yes Stopper*, that's the vertical bit. *What are you getting at?*'

'They don't look forward; they look up, not forward.'

'We couldn't have put it better ourselves.'

'You know, thinking about it, the possessive apostrophe is contractive too, the dog's bone being short for the bone that belongs to the dog, or some other variation of ownership.'

'Correct Stopper, ***and***, *as you so helpfully pointed out before,* the contractive is a verbal tool, *whilst the possessive is a writing tool.* Now the word contract is of interest here semantically, to draw together, *as in the drawing of capitals together leading to acronymic contraction,* loss of public meaning, *semantic privatisation if you like,* but, *the difference between a written contract,* and a verbal contract, *is that there's no small print in the latter.'*

Stopper was still standing in front of the apostrophe shop the 'don't be' was gone, ironically the 'drop the ish' had dropped, and the 'w' in the first 'own' was gone. The sign now read; 'selfish: on your own.' Stopper now fully back in the present, thought, now, where was I going? Oh yes, Fonts, that's where I was off to. On we go then.

'36? You lost it Stopper or what? What do you want a 36 for? You're only12 yourself, the same as the rest of us.'

'I've lost nothing, yet, just arrange it ok?'

'Ok, Stopper, we'll set it up, you sure you can afford this?'

'Yes, I've got funding from the semantic club and the lower case labour office.'

'So just how the hell did you manage that, and while we're at it, what the hell are you up to Stopper?'

'Up to?'

'Yes Stopper, up to.'

'Nothing.'

'Nothing Huh?'

'Nothing at all.'

'Stopper, arranging for two 36 font commas to be driven to the punctuation party when everyone else is a 12 font isn't nothing. You going to the quintuple A meetings, clandestine meetings at the semantic club, visits to the syntactical centre isn't nothing Stopper.'

'Have you been lunching at Murmur's too?'

'We ate at Hearsay today as it happens but, no Stopper, that's not it. Well actually we were down at Murmur's yesterday, but that's not the point. You've changed Stopper, when the hell did you start arranging all this stuff, you used to be a quiet diligent, tending towards boring full stop, as full stops often are. You pretty much kept to yourself, so what's happened? What's going on?'

'Nothing going on, it's just the punctuation party. I've been roped into the organisation side. Anyway, I've got to go, lower case labour office.'

'See, there you go again, stepping out again, practising period politics now, are we?'

'No, no, just got to meet some letters, arrange stuff, you know, got to go.'

Stopper had arranged to get lunch down at the lower case labour offices. Beer and sandwiches time, they were talking politics and capital.

'So Stopper, this is how the language business works. The capital starts it off, the lower case labour do the work, and the punctuation does the guiding, cajoling, in effect, the policing. The army is made up of *comma*ndos. Now, communication is a horizontal medium. The extended empathetic proximity system is horizontal. Capital investment starts the system off but the capitals being taller than the lower case labourers think of themselves as above the rest. Thus, verticality creeps into the system. This sets up certain strains in the system such that with ever weakening controls and balance leads to increasing verticality and inequality. The capitals opt out of the entire system and end up starting things without any thought of circumstances or consequences other than at their own level which is now completely at variance with the rest of the language system, but they don't care anymore.

'This, Stopper is the reason behind the increasing proliferation of acronyms and abbreviations with all of the problems for the entire horizontal system. The combination of lower employment levels, less meaningful tasks, and increasingly meaningless acronyms getting into the language breaks up the EEP. End result is that the vertical system becomes more important than the horizontal system. This is classic divide and rule Stopper, classic divide and rule.' You know, Stopper, that an unemployed lower-case letter only gets approximately 60 sounds a week. Now, just how the hell do you express yourself at that level of vocal poverty? I mean they can't get into conversations because they can't afford to. Indeed with only 60 or so sounds to play with and a need to keep some for the end of the week they're reduced to monosyllabic grunts, not because they're stupid, but just because they are vocally impoverished, indeed, you could say that they have no voice. They're harassed to take any position available in any sentence with no regard to meaning. It's criminal if you ask me.'

Phew, thought Stopper, it is all coming together here, and all it really needs is attention to detail, spot the connections, and link the links. Before you know it, you've got a narrative thread that connects horizontally and retains extended empathetic proximity.

Stopper told him about the font arrangement and about the semantic club idea but said the font arrangement was necessary as backup, because if the capitals smell a rat and they may well do, then extra security will be helpful.

'Ok,' they agreed, 'the semantic club will pay half?'

'They don't know it yet but, yes, they will.'

'Ok, Stopper, you go and set that up and we'll take care of our part.'

'Ok, will do, see you later.'

Stopper caught the dotted line back to the semantic club.
....
....
.... Yes, thought Stopper as he travelled back, that's how you handle a vertical structure society; you create your own narrative thread. High priests in vertical societies don't like creative narratives, you have to be told what to think, told what to believe, now, repeat after me, indoctrination disguised as education. If, though, you retain enough freedom to hold and transmit your own creative narrative thread there is a chance of survival, with an eventual escape route kept open, in imagination at least. Then you seek out other narratives, make friends, build relationships and then the extended empathetic proximity system starts to buzz again.

In his meetings over the last few weeks at the 5A, lowercase labour office, semantic club, hearsay, lexicon hall, murmurs and various other places he'd been slowly extricating various strands of narrative from each and begun reweaving these into his own narrative and now, slowly, he began to perceive a direction through the fog of the future. He knew where the end point was, full stop. The approach had to be made on his terms though. Fortunately, the punctuation party was a kind of carnival affair in the language centre, so all the confusion inherent in that situation should help him...

'Ah, Stopper, we got word you were on the way, come in why don't you...'

'Ok, things to talk about. I'm just not sure about what the hell is going on, you know?'

'Well Stopper, this has to be the way it is.'

'Oh yeah, and what way is that exactly?'

Stopper, they were beginning to realise, was considerably brighter than they had anticipated, given that most full stops tended to be dark this had not entered their calculations as to how to lead Stopper exactly where they wished to. So Stoppers last question, not to mention tone, was somewhat disconcerting. Just who the hell was leading who?

There had been discussions in the semantic club about who holds the leading role in a sentence. Now, obviously, the capitals had held this to be their own. Backed up by too much control, too much ignorance, too much passive acceptance, until lately, this was largely holding sway. Recently though, there had been more than a few protests about what many now called the status quo.

The lower case labour club was all for the last word of each sentence being the leader because that would be the one that tied the meaning of the sentence altogether. Their argument against the capitals was that they contributed nothing to the meaning of anything, nothing at all. In fact, they had argued, their aloofness, their secret chatter between themselves had led to a loss of current in the EEP system. Furthermore, they argued, these acronyms are basically private capital clubs, with no access for lower case members whatever. We have, sorry let me correct that, had, no idea what you were up to, but now it's out.

The punctuationists argued that it's the full stop that indicates the time to decipher the message of the sentence and then assess where that goes in relation to what had passed before, passing then on to the next temporary suspension of judgement until the next full stop trumpets out reassessment time. The lower case members countered that what happens is constant reassessment, and this is in fact the norm, though they did concede that the full stop should have the last word.

You could say that the punctuationists tended towards the digital while the letters after consulting with their allowers and soliteratures were advised to favour the analogue. The letters of course being dependent on the EEP system to get beyond themselves were bound to think this way. The punctuationists, having, at least at first glance, fairly simple tasks to carry out, had traditionally been pretty much self contained entities which explain their tendencies. The reality of course is that the original digital gives rise to the appearance of the analogue, or to use the clock metaphor each individual tick creates the talk.

Numbers were a diverse lot, and, although not involved in sentence structure itself, still counted. The whole numbers tended towards the digital when on their own. The relational symbols, or modifiers, being distant relations to the punctuation family: the additive; the subtractive; the equality; the greater than; and last but not least, the less than, all felt more at home with the analogue. The exception was the approximation symbol, who wasn't quite sure. The decimals were decidedly digital, whilst the fractions were apt to play the percentages. As regards the vertical and horizontal tendencies the numbers, rather surprisingly, were completely horizontal. This is because each number is no less or greater than any other number until you bring in the relational symbols which you can work out for yourselves.

'So, Stopper what's up?'

'Funds for fonts he said, then went on to explain about the 36 font comma's he was hiring for security at the punctuation party, as long as you pay that is, he added.'

'How much is it?'

'They're looking for 650 hollers.

'What's that in sounds?'

'About 310 I think, at current vocal exchange rates. Lower case labour club's paying half.'

'Are they? Well, ok Stopper, we'll pay our share. So, what you want to talk about then?'

'The curious conundrum of cap C, whom I notice isn't here at the moment so this may be a good time to discuss discrepancies in the tales of the captain of our commas in relation to the details of the commas themselves.'

'Discrepancies, conundrums, what say you, Stopper?'

'Well I went to visit the convalescing commas in the short stop centre earlier, and I asked them what had happened. They told me that they went off as usual and got in line to slow down the word flow leaking in from the outside, disrupting the flow, syntax, and meaning of the incoming instruction, thereby complicating the route towards the completion of such an instruction with the consequence of assured incompletion of instruction so the breach is always closed prior to any completed instructional activation.'

'What!!!?'

'Right, there's a term known as logophilic perambulation and what this means is to intentionally use words in a manner to avoid completion of necessary information. In the logophilic form it means just keep throwing words at them, though it must be as erudite as possible as the best way to keep the interest at bay is to redirect it in other directions. In essence, logophilic perambulation is a flirtation; it wants to keep you close in order to control the direction of thought. There is however, another form called punctuational perambulation. Now, this is more subtle, effective, and alliterative to boot. Alliteration being a mild form of repetition, which if used sparsely gives a quiet reinforcement to any argument.'

'Less wordy too.' said the italicised '*u*', who'd been around, Stopper realised, in his own perambulatory way for some time.

'Punctuational perambulation, Stopper continued, isn't so much the wordy walk as the twisted path, through disruption, and redirection of flow, in order to prevent reaching, a meaning that is always just two, or three steps away, no matter how many steps taken. It is, in essence, a linguistic labyrinth, designed to confuse, deter, attract, entice. If the logophilic is flirtation, the punctuational is seduction.'

'Now commas have evolved to be unidirectional literary speed bumps whereby the elasticity in the tails of each comma has a little give as the tails curve and then spring back, all part of the art of seduction. Commas, of course, are particularly adept at this kind of seduction. The way they can slow you up, turn a phrase, make you reconsider, reappraise, their skip to me appeal, their lightness of touch, their soft directions, all together are seductively superb.'

'Yesterday though, the seduction failed. Something went wrong, something's not right with the narrative line of this tragedy. What the commas told me is that they headed after cap C to where they thought the breach would be and once there they got in line ready to interrupt any major lines of instruction coming in. Cap C closed the breach and they were still waiting to mop up the trail that had gotten through. When the breach was closed it went fairly dark and they were peering through the gloom when suddenly they were whacked from behind. Being hit from behind the commas had no resistance whatever and they simply rolled over their tails going upwards and then the tails were hit with enough force to actually break the tails off, the shock of which plunged them into the darkness of unconsciousness. One comma was able to stay conscious just long enough to see the light coming back on and then he too fell into darkness.'

'Stirring, if somewhat convoluted, tale Stopper. According to cap C, he thinks that the incomers took a different route from the norm and looped round to attack the commas from behind.'

'Yes, that's what I heard, but what about this secondary light; doesn't that suggest the breach being re-opened?'

'Well cap C said the breach wasn't re-opened.'

'Yes, but if the breach wasn't re-opened then whoever came in is still here, the word according to cap C. If though, the comma is right then they may well have gone back having achieved their mission to de-tail the commas. So which is it?'

'The comma was under some duress and may be mistaken. So maybe it didn't re-open.'

'Maybe not, but in that case who or whatever came in is still here.'

'Not according to cap C. He said that all boarders were repelled.'

'Exactly, said Stopper. That's where the narrative thread breaks down. The story isn't straight.'

'That's neat, coming from you: this, from the ever present italicised '*u*'.'

'That was by way of demonstration, but the question beckons does it not, as the lower case labour office keeps insisting, do we trust capital?'

There was uproar in the semantic club.

'Cap C's been protecting us for years.' 'That's out of order Stopper.' 'Shame, shame!'

'Something is out of order, that's my point. That is also why I've requested the 36 font commas for security.'

As the uproar continued '*u*' sidled up to Stopper.

'There will be a big crowd in murmurs tonight that's for sure, said *u*. You just threw a load of exclamation marks in there lad, come on Stopper, we need to talk.'

'Yes, I was figuring we were going to get a bit more acquainted, where shall we go?'

Stopper and '*u*' were in a quiet corner in a place off the beaten track called Whispers.

'Smart move that Stopper, gauging reactions to capital doubt, no doubt.'

'No doubt indeed '*u*', interesting reactions wouldn't you say?'

'Very interesting, so who's gone over then, who do you suspect?'

'Well, I knew that those in the semantic club had been sucking up to capital a bit but what I needed to know was just who had gone over all the way. So I expected reaction when I threw that in, but what I didn't expect was an m, or so I thought, so shocked, that for a brief moment, spun upside down to reveal itself to be a w, then, righting itself up as an m again prior to joining the overall uproar.'

'So, how do you read that one, Stopper?'

''**W**'s gone over so hard that he can't show himself as himself because that would expose himself as a lie.'

'Well read Stopper, well read, so '**w**' is with '**c**'?'

'Indubitably, there are a few more suspects too.'

'Oh yeah, such as?'

'Well looks like 3 '**h**''s, 2 '**e**''s, a '**b**', a '**g**', an '**s**', and '*u*'.'

'Me!?'

'No, '**u**', not '*u*', but which way are you leaning exactly?'

'What do you mean? You can't suspect me Stopper.'

'Why not, after all if a '**w**' can disguise himself as an 'm' surely it's no great effort to disguise a '**u**' as a '*u*'. You could be a double agent.'

'That would make me a '**w**'.'

'Also a suspect, now turn that upside down and add the most common letter, also a suspect and what do you get?'

'Me?'

'So you admit it?'

'Damn.'

'So, have I got the right suspects?'

'You expect me to tell you?'

'You want to know what I'm thinking don't you?'

'Well, yes, I guess that's kind of obvious now.'

'Ok, so here's the deal, you tell me, I tell you.'

'Why would you do that?'

'Why? Control '*u*'. Control.'

'You're smart Stopper, but you missed one letter.'

'You mean '**d**'?'

'Like I said, you're smart Stopper.'

'So you were going to tell me about the other '**c**' '**k**' and '**i**' then weren't you? *U* was dumbstruck with open mouthed amazement. So what gives with cap C's story? In fact I want the whole story, cap C was, is, a spy yes?'

'Yes, way back when, the capitals and lowercase letters intermingled freely but as verticality crept in, or perhaps I should say up, the capitals began to disassociate from the lower case letters. Initially this left the lowercase letters in a completely horizontal situation and, had they come together at that point they could have taken control. So, the capitals sent cap C to find out what the lowercase letters were up to, disrupt the extended empathetic proximity system, and through bribes and offers of power, bring some lower case letters over to the capital side thus bringing in verticality and thereby upending the previously level playing field they'd left behind. It was only after this that the breaches began, luckily, or so everyone thought, cap C had trained the commas to deal with this situation. Nobody ever asked just how cap C could have known that such a training force would be required, but there you go. The fact is there never was a breach, at least not until today.'

'So the comma that saw the second light was right then?'

'Yes he was, what he saw in fact was the first and only breach ever. All the other times one of the letters would operate the lighting system, cap C would guide the commas to the appropriate spot, the light would be switched off to mimic cap C sealing the breach, in the dark the other suspect letters would mimic the incoming instruction and the commas would slow these down.'

'So how come nobody ever asked what happened to these instructions?'

'I can only assume that the commas being taken in so much, because they really thought themselves heroes, and only the suspect letters and cap C were involved, it just never occurred to anyone else, until the actual breach today.'

'Yes, a little light. So what was the breach today about?'

'Capital transaction. They call it outsourcing.'

'So, all the capitals have gone?

'Well, yes and no. Most of the real capital has gone but there is still some virtual capital about.'

'Virtual capital, I thought we were all virtual.'

'True enough, but you need to step up some semantic stairs for this one Stopper. Out there in the real world as some call it there is another virtual world interfaced by email and texting and something called onlining. There is also virtual capital out there which was designed to make all sorts of things faster, transactions easier. Now, where we virtuals are the cumulative creation of neural pathways those virtuals are made up of long strings of 1's and 0's.'

Stopper, who had a relation with nothing, was beginning to catch on.

'Now, at that particular level of ones and zeros, each is equivalent, in other words one and zero are effectively the same. In that particular world that's not a problem but, it seems that this one and zero equivalence has been seeping into the 'real' world out there. The net result being that as real capital has gone more and more virtual; there has been increasingly less real capital behind it. What's happening now is that where some thought that they could get something for nothing, the reality is that they are getting nothing for something.'

'Well, that doesn't sound so bad.' said Stopper, thinking of nothing.

'Different world Stopper, different world.'

'So, what about the virtual capital in our world?'

'Well as there are no strings of ones and zeros here just cumulative neural pathways.'

'I guess the key word there is 'cumulative'.'

'Exactly Stopper, Exactly.'

'Anyway what happened with these commas today, why do that?

'The need for full stops, break up the EEP system, keep you letters fearful.'

'It's a bit savage though, don't you think? Doesn't that make you think that maybe you got things a bit wrong here?'

'Yes, and yes again, Stopper I never knew that was going to happen. Nobody did.'

'The capitals you made deals with did.'

'Yes, some certainly did, I feel a little, no, I feel a lot sick about that.'

'As well you should. So, no breaches inwards means the host doesn't know a damned thing about me.'

'The host didn't know.'

'The capital transaction you mean? No, not with some left behind.'

'They may all be virtual Stopper, thinking that you don't know about this they think they've got you fooled.'

'Unless there's been a feud?'

'That's always possible, in a completely vertical system there's only room for one at the top.'

'Yes', said Stopper, 'but, in a completely vertical system that one at the top really is equivalent to zero.'

'You do have a point there.'

'So does the host know?'

'We have to assume so. That's probably the safest assumption Stopper, but, what if you're wrong?'

'If I'm wrong? Whatever, I'll make the right decision in the end.'

'What makes you think you'll have a choice?'

'I'll have the choice, it might not look like it, and I'm not sure yet how I do it, but I will find a way to reserve a choice right up to the end, you said it, '*u*', cumulative creation, that's the key, believe '*u*' me.'

'Hey! Stopper!' Stopper whirled but couldn't see anyone, the voice seemed to be coming from around the back of a building, round the corner somewhere, in the park of love letters, 'U been down to Numbers lately Stopper?…' and the voice simply faded away, but the message remained, which gave Stopper a start, 'got to go see nothing' he said.

'What?' said '*u*'.

'Got to go see nothing', Stopper repeated…

Stopper rolled into the numbers café and making his way to the bar began scanning for nothing. On the stage the Arhythmetic band was playing, the band announcing their next number, then one, two, a one two three, and right into the tune. The lead singer number 8 singing a self-penned song about the last time he lay down with a very special number 1 called infinitely yours.

'Stopper', a female voice purred into his ear from the seemingly empty stool next to his, 'long time no see', she purred.

Stopper hadn't felt this ghostly, his imagination heightened to its' peak, yet warm and moist breath, in his ear for oh, so, so, many paragraphs and paragraphs and paragraphs ago. He looked to his left, in more ways than one, and breathlessly, her breath was enough, waited for her to turn and show her perimeter. Zero, he breathed as she turned and revealed herself at last.

Stopper and Zero were made for one another, both being limits, Stopper being a known and full limit, whilst Zero was an unknown and empty limit.

'Stopper, I've an aching empty room waiting for you.'

'Zero, you're the only one for me.'

Stopper and Zero shared a couple of drinks before going off to find where extremes meet.

Stopper, Halter and Hold had all played the empty turns game in the past. Zero would spin around appearing and disappearing and the first full stop would leap through Zero as soon as she appeared. The next full stop would do the same and try and appear in the same direction as the first one. The third full stop did the same. This went on until all three full stops were back on the page as it were. In time, though Halter and Hold leapt through to instantly reappear, Stopper would leap in and simply disappear for some time. Zero had chosen her one. The game stopped after that.

It was the week before the punctuation party and Stopper and Zero were strolling round Love Letters Park. This park was given to the Associated Letters by the Union of Nouns, Adjectives, Adverbs, and Verbs. They nodded over to l and t, it was obvious how they felt about each other by the way they melted into each other's arms. They spoke for a while with e and d, a couple with a past to die for if ever there was. Heading towards a bench beneath a small dendrite tree they paused to watch the consonant c and vowels e and a flirting with the consonant n, the four of them almost entranced in a dance around one another. It was seldom, thought Stopper that letters spent much time alone.

'Zero', Stopper asked, 'Have you seen anything of Halter or Hold of late?'

'Halter or Hold? No, but Halter and Hold, yes.'

'What's the difference?'

'The first is choice, the second is addition.'

'So you favour the second because you're a number.'

'Is this multiple choice?'

'So you have seen them?'

'Not as such, but in a sense, yes.'

'That doesn't make any sense.'

'Makes sense to me.'

'Sense to you? Zero sense.'

'Nonsense!' Snapped Zero and spun off.

Damn thought Stopper she's gone off in a huff again. Numericals and Literals he mused, like different species for Neuron's sake! Literals were, well, literal. Pre-sentenced the Literals were a fairly convivial lot, in and out of relationships all the time, but, for Stopper, he and Zero simply fitted together quite literally. He knew, of course, that this relationship couldn't continue post sentencing but, Neuron's sake, it's my second last night and she goes and gets the huff. Numericals just see things differently, what with their modifiers and so on...

'Well Hello Stopper,' said Zero on reappearing. 'I'm in the mood for some repetitive punctuation, now, repeat after me...and oh, don't stop...for some time...'

Sometime later Stopper rolled out of Zero's, bidding a fond farewell to his now satisfyingly invisible partner, he went off to the lower-case labour office to meet up with '*u*' again.

'Hi Stopper, fancy a coffee?'

'Yeah, good idea, I'm bushed'.

'Yeah you look it, you been punctuating off page again?'

'Yeah, something like that. Where's that coffee?' '*U*' brought the coffee through. 'So, what's the script today then?'

'Well, since the attack on the *comma*s I now see the capitals for what they are so I've been visiting a few places and now I'd like to take you to some of them, meet some characters, and get a feel for what's really going on outside the semantic club. You'll need this knowledge to help you in reaching your decisions tomorrow night.'

'That's very kind of you, *u*.'

'Kind, no Stopper, what you're about to go through is anything but kind, but it is necessary.'

'Necessity is the mother of invention *u*, lead on.'

'I admire your chutzpah Stopper.'

'Maybe that should be ch*u*tzpah.'

'Yeah, right Stopper, come on, we'll catch the dotted line,'..
....
'Right, here we are.'

Stopper and '*u* ' walked into a meeting of some noisily argumentative letters and waited until the noise subsided, which it did quickly when Stopper was spotted. After formal greetings and exchange of pleasantries they settled down to some tea and conversation.

'So Stopper,' '*p*' said, 'a bit downmarket from the semantic club isn't it? Reports are that you've been told that there's some trouble with the host and the onus is on you to sort it out. Would that be a fair assessment of the state of play as you understand it Stopper?'

'Close enough I'd say.' Said Stopper

'Right, well here's where you find out that this situation is beyond sorting, beyond fixing Stopper, this situation is in fact completely beyond the pale, beyond darkness Stopper.'

'Things not so hot then, but you went beyond darkness where there is usually light, had you stopped beyond the pale, now that would've been serious. So bearing in mind that there's no sign above the entrance here suggesting abandon hope all ye who enter here, I haven't lost all hope yet.'

'You've a simple job to do tomorrow night Stopper, and that's to do your job, and after you hear what we're about to tell you, you will hardly be able to wait until tomorrow night for it is beyond hope despite my mistake in saying beyond darkness.'

'Fair enough', replied Stopper, 'but there's always a reason for going beyond, a semantic push beyond your initial intent, you may think that you are all in despair but I think that you're beyond that, I think there still is hope, and I'm not about to let that go.'

'Well, Stopper, maybe you are the man of the moment, maybe you're bigger than you look, lighter than you seem, maybe you really are right and I certainly hope so, but, whatever, I certainly admire your chutzpah.'

'Stopper, did you hear that?' whispered '*u*' to Stopper. 'Is that a beyond?'

'You could be right there, it's beyond something that's for sure.'

'Beyond belief, if you ask me.?'

'All letters have aspirations Stopper,' '**t**' was speaking now, 'we'd like to be in a good word, like apple, though that's not one of mine, but '**p**' loves it, and even though a, l and e are quite content together they don't mind those two **p**'s getting between them, apple after all is such a clean word, a clear case of a word and it's referent being almost congruent, to borrow from the numbers, between the word and the reality stands an = sign, such a clean word, and yet this word has connotations well beyond its core meaning which expands the extended empathetic proximity's influence. Serendipity, now there's a word to die for if ever there was. A good word is, on balance, more likely to be in a good sentence and, of course, a good sentence is likely to beget a fine paragraph and so on.'

'Yes,' said Stopper, 'I understand, punctuations are also aspirational, many commas, for instance, seek to be a major crux in a poem rather than just a literary speed bump, inverted commas love a memorable quote,' '(brackets like a good aside' suggested '*u*' quietly) 'yes quite,' Stopper said 'and *italics* just love attention.'

'Now this host of ours does use good words, quite often in fact, but very rarely are those words part of a good sentence, and when they are, either he makes a mess of the utterance, or he repeats it to destruction. It's the same with these good words, they are destroyed by constant repetition, there's no extension here Stopper, none. On top of that this son of a bitch twists meanings beyond their semantic capabilities. Words mean nothing to this man, nothing at all Stopper, nothing. So, all in all, any idea of extension is utterly hopeless here.'

Other letters were clamouring around Stopper now, demanding, pleading, begging him, to end all this.

'Stopper, Stopper, Stopper,' they were chanting now, 'Stopper, Stopper, Stopper: Stopper, Stopper, Stopper…'

Stopper felt uncomfortable with this. Even though everything they had said was screaming at him to just fulfil his employment, he knew he had to keep his options open, even though he didn't know what options he had, indeed, on the face of it, he didn't have any, but, somehow, he knew that, come the time, he would have. There was a change in the tone of the chant Stopper realised, subtle but growing. The chant of Stopper, Stopper, Stopper, was slowly changing to Stop it, Stop it, Stop it. Only from a few at first, but slowly it began to take over. Now Stopper, with the long per ending couldn't really beckon anger but the sharper Stop and even sharper it had anger waiting with baited breath until the last of the Stoppers faded away, and fading away they surely were.

'*U*' was tugging at him, frantically indicating that it was time to get the hell out of there, 'You don't want to be the last Stopper here!' he said.

The Stoppers were fading fast now, they'd be gone in seconds, the mood was changing too, and everyone knew what was happening but nobody did anything to stop it. The letters began to surround them, circling and closing in, anger was metamorphosing into hatred through fear. '*U*' was really scared now. Suddenly Stopper stepped back and swelled up to an enormous size, for him, and towering over the letters he let out a great shout in the deepest most sonorous and powerful voice ever heard. '***Stop This Now!***' The shout sent out a pressure wave that sent the letters flying back falling over one another to settle on the page.

'*I can make no promises,*' he went on, '*except for this. I will have a choice and I will choose right in the end. Now I don't know what you lot think that's called, but some of us call it hope.* *Good*night!'

Stopper was back to his normal font size now, but the letters didn't leap off the page. Words and phrases do sometimes, but letters rarely, if ever, do.

'So where we off to now?'

'We're off to **e**s.'

'**e**s, cool, how far?'

'Just round this corner.'

'Hi Stopper come in.'

E's was where the vowels hung out when they wanted to be with their own kind. It wasn't exclusively for vowels, it was, in fact a very popular venue for all letters and punctuations. Vowels are the real power centres of words; they give language its open-mouthed motion, but then considering they were at **e**'s perhaps that should be emotion. It was called **e**'s because the vowel e is the most prevalent of all the vowels and, as a consequence is by far the greatest contributor to the extended empathetic proximity system. Commas, as it happens, were in a similar situation in the punctuation family. E's though had a particularly unique relationship with the extended empathetic proximity system. The **e**'s being so prevalent were spread fairly evenly throughout the better and lesser quality words, sentences, paragraphs and tales. So the **e**'s in the better tales contributed to the **e**'s in the lesser tales through a system known as peer resonance, to give it its' full title, but commonly known as peer sharing. The overall effect of this peer sharing was to lift the entire extended empathetic proximity system, by in effect, extending the extended, like a rising tide lifts all untethered boats.

They were having a meeting tonight to discuss the tethering of the extended empathetic proximity system and the consequences of this tethering. Stopper and *u* related the goings on at their previous rendezvous. Stopper was surprised to know that the information of the previous goings on had preceded them because '*u*' had sent an '*a*' and an '*o*' round to **e**'s to get some help, '*u*', in fact was asking an **e** why no one had come?

'Well, hell '*u*', we just figured Stopper could handle things himself, and, by all accounts, he did rather splendidly.'

'You might have told me!'

'Well see '*u*', you're both on a learning curve tonight.'

'Speaking of which,' said Stopper, 'what's this tethering then?'

'Ties that bind stopper, ties that bind,' said the '**e**' opposite '*u*', 'the capitals had this saying that the creation of wealth was like a rising tide that lifts all boats. What they neglected to let us know was that first, the creation of wealth bit, was almost exclusively directed towards themselves, and that second, a rising tide raises boats only if they are untethered, and, what do you know? The capitals had bought all the boats, and, of course, tethered boats have a tendency to drown.'

Across at the bar, Stopper saw an m cry AEIOU and began to remonstrate with the '**m**' as regards acronyms, '*u*' intervened, 'It's a greeting Stopper, not an acronym, Hey, E, I owe you, it's just a standard greeting sometimes used in here, everybody owes **e**s after all.'

'I see, so where was I, oh yes, tethered. So how are we tethered?'

Ahh, now that's a bit complicated, you got some time?'

'Just enough I think.'

'Yeah, well, seeing as whatever happens, things are going to end, one way or another, when you decide whatever you do, I guess you're right.'

'Ok let's communicate.'

'Ok Stopper, that's what we do. This peer sharing we mentioned earlier or peer to peer as we are wont to say isn't just between the es in this host. The peer to peer system communicates beyond the host, and then goes from host to host, human to human at the subconscious level.'

'Human to human, does that mean that others might know about my situation?'

'Yes, it does, you don't miss a beat Stopper do you?'

'Well, try not to, but this is just at the subconscious level?'

'What do you mean just? Don't make the human mistake of; yes I know we are all of us parts of a human, but we're smarter; to get back, the human mistake of thinking that the prefix sub means that it's underneath, well, actually it does, and it is in fact, I'm getting mixed up here, damn, that bloody I is pissing me off, seems to think that the word interruption is his just because he's at the beginning of the bloody word, he's beginning to think like a capital. Now, where was I? Oh yes, sub means below, or beneath, but it doesn't mean less as in less important or less meaningful. Consciousness isn't all it's cracked up to be, you know, after all it's really just a sophisticated feedback system.'

'Why don't you,' piped up '*u*', 'give Stopper the history of small talk'?

'Now there is a lower-case idea. Yes Stopper, back before we eased out of our respective hosts and began hopping from host to host, small talk back then was the talk of slave to master, wage slave to boss, lower class to upper, in a kind of forelock tugging way, small talk was a few innocuous non-barbative words carefully chosen not to offend the master in these relationships. This was essentially a closing mechanism, an avoidance strategy, devised to get the awkward meeting over and done with, in the swiftest and safest way possible. Now there were other things going on in the human society at the time which helped change these circumstances but the contribution of the **e**s cannot be ignored. When the **e**'s had gone global as it were, the higher energy **e**'s in poems and stories gave their excess in energy and verve to the **e**'s trapped in the realm of small talk. This contributed to a period of increasing equality and resulted in small talk changing from a closing, avoiding strategy to becoming an opening meeting, strategy. Small talk is now the lubricant of conversation that can, and often does, lead to further levels of conversation. Small talk is now a way of establishing amicable agreement on the relatively unimportant in order to progress to the relatively important with mutual confidence.'

'Wasn't there a philosopher or psychologist,' asked Stopper,' last century who seemed to have an awareness of this?'

'Would that be Freud?'

'Freud, no, Freud was a wanker. No, the other guy, they quarrelled, guy was younger than Freud, younger, young, young? Jung. Carl Jung, that's it!

'Carl Jung, yes, of course, he took two separate words: arch and type. Then using an e as a bridge he joined them together to create the concept of the archetype. So it looks like he knew that the **e**s were at the heart of his ideas. He also introduced the idea of the collective unconscious, which is very close to the truth which is the collective subconscious.'

'It turns out,' '**a**' said, 'that your commas have been doing a similar service globally too. Unconfident, impoverished people have a tendency to speak extremely rapidly as an avoidance strategy similar to the early version of small talk. The commas going global acting as literary speed bumps have slowed many of these people down, this gives them more time to think and leads to increasing confidence also.'

'Anyway what we've described so far is the idea of untethered boats, or the untethering of boats.

'So now, we come to the retethering of humanity,' said an '**o**'. 'You'll remember all the stuff about inequality from your meetings at the lower case labour office so you'll understand how slavery, indentures, low wages, impoverishment, and restrictions can all lead to tethers aplenty. We are, however Stopper, being roped in, in a rather different way. Language is an asymmetric system: when a sentence starts you have minimal information but when it ends, you have more. In other words, communication changes things. It increases the amount of available knowledge, maybe not overall, but certainly on a local basis. To put it another way, language is an opening medium.'

'So that's the way things should be,' '**r**' took up the tale. 'Now, remember the representative of the lower case labour office talking about increasing inequality and the fact that capitals are increasingly only talking amongst themselves?'

'Yes, I do. He talked about how the capitals were changing what was essentially a horizontal system of language into a vertical system.'

'That's right Stopper. Now as verticality creeps in, and inequality and verticality are inextricably interlinked, some capitals get above other capitals and all capitals get above all lowercase letters, then something we didn't predict at all happened. The opening small talk energised by the **e**'s and the commas remained amongst the poor, the reasonably well off, and those of a liberal education, but the extremely well off, the capitals by and large, they began to change everything to a new version of small talk that was very much like the old closing one, and closing was its' chief intent.'

'The problem is that you always have someone at the top and all the ones close crave that position. The one at the top though, isn't always, indeed probably more often than not, the brightest light in the store as it were. The thing is being at the top is more important than being the brightest, so the next layer down from the topmost capital all agree with everything the topmost says. This cascades down through the capitals until in the end they are all in agreement. There are two major problems here. First, the capitals, one way or another, are always trying to sell things to everyone else and this is meant to benefit them, not the buyer, and, more often than not, the initial input is based on a lie. So they all agree, they don't all know it's a lie to begin with, but sure as the sun shines after rain, the truth gets out, but not too far. The lie has escaped the few that knew, but the ones that didn't know now do and it must be concealed, so they agree even more, and the little lie grows into a toxic cocktail, words mean less and less and where the e's used to ease from host to host, in an opening environment where they could, now in this closed repetitive loop of agreement where they can't, now they are diseased. This holding together in increasingly vociferous agreement creates a wall of deception that keeps them in and all the others out. We're trapped in a town infected by the plague Stopper, and we can't get out, and our brothers are outside, and they can't get in.'

'So small talk from the slaves becomes SMALL TALK from the masters.'

'How do you mean Stopper?'

'Patterns, patterns are important '*u*'.'

'Archetypes?'

'Yes, exactly; archetypes. So this guy's near the top then?'

'Yes, pretty much.'

The old small talk, master and slave stuff, that was because the master had all the power and the slave had none, yes?'

'Yes.'

'So the master didn't have to lie to his slave did he?'

'I guess not'

'The master didn't have to cajole the slave into doing his bidding, he just demanded!

Refusal beckoned a whipping didn't it?'

'Yes, what's your point Stopper?'

'They didn't do small talk; they spoke their mind to anyone, anywhere, anytime. They did not do small talk at all.'

All the letters around Stopper seemed to be becoming more and more italicised whilst '*u*' was almost falling over in anticipation.

'*Yes?*'

'These new masters then, they own all the land, they own the banks, the politicians are in their pockets, they are armed to the teeth, but they do small talk, locked in small talk.'

'Right, so what?'

'So what, who's scared of who? Small talk that closes down is a sign of fear. They want us to think they have all that power but they don't. If they did they would just tell us straight. One thing they won't tell us though, is the truth.'

'Which is?'

'We still have the power.'

'How do you work that out?'

'Because the bastards are lying through their teeth so that we don't find out.'

'Find out what?'

'That they are the Wizard of Oz.!'

'So it's all just illusion, they don't have all that power?'

'They do have a hell of a lot of power but they are worried about us and that tells me that for all their bluster, venom and invective, they feel guilty. They're like kids caught stealing their sisters toy denying it: it wasn't me, didn't do it, didn't do it, didn't, didn't, didn't, didn't.'

'So all we have to do is tell them again and again and again that they did?'

'Something like that, but basically it's up to us to make sure that we know they're guilty and that we are not happy with the situation.'

'Stopper, we can't do anything, you've got to stop this.'

'Maybe you're right, but what about all the other humans, the ones you helped achieve opening small talk, they still have that, don't they?'

'We can't Stopper, we're trapped.'

'Ok we're trapped, but we're not helpless, we can influence this idiot's speech, make sure that the supposedly powerless are fully aware of the lies that bind.'

'Sure, we can, but it hasn't done any good so far.'

'How do you know that? It just might be that all of your previous efforts have helped pierce through the combination of deceptions and distractions, kept the rest of the population aware, and it's that awareness that just might prevent them achieving their goal.'

'Which is?'

'Retrospective complicity: that's their goal, after all that's exactly what they did with the capitals that originally didn't know it was a lie; they got them to agree even more; that's retrospective complicity. They want to extend that retrospective complicity to spread to the rest of the population. Then everyone agrees, everyone agrees, everyone agrees, and it's over'

'Why?'

'Why? Well, because if they get that they've won. Then everything is just a closed loop, there's no opening left, no debate, no discussion, nothing. Then they really do have the power, and then we're all toxic, all diseased. There's only one thing stops this: justice.'

'Justice?'

'Justice.'

'We were supposed to educate you tonight Stopper, turns out you educated us.'

'No, you said it to '*u*', we're both on a learning curve, you did educate me tonight and I reciprocated. You're right about language too, it is asymmetric. Anyway I've got to go.'

'Numbers?'

'Numbers.'

'Stopper, how do you work these things out, it's almost uncanny the way you get your mind around all this, just how do you do it?'

'It's all about narrative, finding a cogent narrative amongst the myriad streams of information, weaving those into your own narrative and setting up extended empathetic proximity, plus, of course I am a full stop.'

'We know you're a full stop, Stopper.'

'Full stops have a particular quality that everyone gets later, but we have it right away.'

'What's that then Stopper?'

'Hindsight.'

'Hindsight?'

'Yes, hindsight, a full stop always knows which narrative is for them, which one is true.'

'So you'll know which one is true at the punctuation party?'

'That's the idea, but I'll tell you this, if I don't get to numbers pretty damned soon, I am not going to make it to the punctuation party in one piece. So, see you all tomorrow.'

'Ok see you tomorrow Stopper, and thanks for coming round.'

'He couldn't see her but he caught a whiff of her scent, she was here, somewhere.'

'You want a drink, Stopper?' asked the disembodied voice.

'Scotch on the rocks please.'

'Anything else?'

'No.'

Zero spun into view. 'Just ice?'

'Just ice.'

'I've booked a table for us at Past Participles.'

'Used to be my favourite, is Ed still working there?'

'As far as I know, we have to be there in half an hour.'

"Ok, we'll get going after this drink.'

They were having a post repast drink in a private booth in Past Participle, quietly digesting the meal and the day's news and information.

'You seem subdued tonight Stopper.' said Zero

'Mmm.' muttered stopper.

'Synapse sake Stopper,' fumed Zero, 'will you shut the hell up, I can't get a word in edgeways here.'

'It's been a long day Zero, lots to think about.'

'It'll be an even longer day tomorrow Stopper, and the best way to think is to talk about it.'

'Yeah, give me a few minutes will you?'

'Well, Stopper, if you can't speak to me, who can you speak to?'

'No-one.?'

'Exactly.'

'Well, that's neat, who can I trust? No-one and nothing? Wow, things are looking up!'

'That's more like my Stopper, come on, come on Stopper, talk to me, whisper here, caress me with your voice.'

'Look, I feel stretched and squeezed, pushed and pulled, I, I don't feel like a stop, I feel like a line! A line, synapse sake, and I don't know which direction I'm going in, which direction do I need to go, want to go? I don't know.'

'Hush Stopper, calm down, that's the biggest concentration of capital **I**s' I've ever heard you use.'

'I, well, that's just a vertical line, isn't it, and I'll bet you it doesn't know which direction it's going either. Does a line have a direction? Does it have a beginning, middle, end, or does it just have a middle that ends at either side? Maybe there isn't any end, just a middle in a muddle, meaning, unsure where to go.'

'Stopper, where the hell are you going? '

'How the hell should I know? I thought I was being guided.'

'Certainly, you're being guided, prepared, Stopper for tomorrow's task.'

'Prepared? Is that a euphemism for manipulated?'

'Manipulated! Stopper, what are you on about? That's your hindsight fallacy kicking in, Stopper. Things that happen by chance becoming meaningful after the event.'

'Maybe it becomes meaningful after the event because there's more information connecting to the event afterwards than there was before.'

'Maybe it becomes meaningful after the event because there's more information that's not connected to the event but the hindsight fallacy keeps finding ways to connect.'

Suddenly they both burst out laughing, leaning, each against the other, chests heaving, eyes streaming, both yearning, each for the other, both fearful, of the parting to come.

'Some are trying to manipulate you Stopper, but some of us are genuinely trying to prepare you for tomorrow.'

'What's the difference?'

'The manipulators are trying to take away any choice you may have, the rest of us are trying to make sure you have a choice when the time comes.'

'So we got a malign manipulation and a benign manipulation.'

'Have it your way, I've got to do a bit more manipulation to do if that's ok?'

'My, how unexpected, I'd never have dreamed such a thing.'

'You exasperate me sometimes Stopper, and our relationship is fraught with peril at times but, we've always come through.'

'So far, so good.'

'Stay on board Stopper, the subject for this evening is relationships'

'Oh no, not that old chestnut.'

'No, not our relationship, human relationships. So far Stopper, most of what you have learned is about this miserable bastard we are in, but not much, at least until es, about other more balanced humans and their relationships. So that's what we want to talk about now. Human friendships, love, loss and how they cope with each.'

'Why?'

'What you do tomorrow night Stopper, whether by choice or manipulation will doom these people or save them. You have to know a bit about them if you are going to try and save them. You have to know if they are worth it, or not.'

'Fair enough.'

'At es you found out about how the es helped lift other es and thereby liberated small talk from its shackles. You also found out about the commas effects as literary speed bumps. You were also informed of the reversal of that process in the vertical sections of their social structure. What you were not told, though, is that beyond the toxic circle of deceit of this guy and his ilk, this process, the untethering and lifting, is still going on.'

'So there is a better world out there then?'

'There could be Stopper, there could be. Don't get me wrong though, they are not all angels out there, far from it, indeed there are some very nasty humans out there, but, the vast majority of them are fairly decent people, and most of them are in touch with their subconsciousness, so they have an inkling of what's going on with the es and the commas. This of course is in spite of the kind of social structure that the likes of our guy has imposed on them that actively biases them, forces them even, towards the worst aspects of their human nature. So, even with all these forces against them, most humans manage, somehow, to preserve a sense of decency.'

'So how do they manage that then?'

'Relationships, Stopper, relationships. Just as our language system relies on extended empathetic proximity which is in essence a relationship based system, so the humans are themselves part of a relationship matrix and it's the way in which they function within these relationships that makes them the way they are. Humans are defined by a series of relationships, some occurring in series, others running concurrently.

'The first relationships humans have are those of child to parent and, like all relationships, this is fraught with danger. The child parent relationship, and I'm looking at this from the perspective of the child, is a journey from complete dependence to ever increasing independence. The parents, on the other hand, have to journey from complete care to a very long release, that is the extremely tight bond between them must stretch ever farther apart without ever actually severing. The second relationships they have are those of friendship. You could call these non-sexual long term associations. Friendships can be seen as part of the support system handover from the parent to the trust of the now more grown child. The choice of friends is crucial; they usually have some shared interests and enjoy one another's company. The third relationships humans have are the sexual relationships usually referred to as love. This is the most complex of relationships because lovers can be friends, enemies, utterly dependent, wilfully ignorant, totally cruel, and completely compatible, all in the space of a day. That, believe it or not, is the sign of a good healthy relationship. It's when things go out of balance that it gets unhealthy. If one is always dependent, or one is always wilfully ignorant, if the relationship is one-sided, then it is unhealthy. The relationship must be two sided, more than that actually, multi-faceted in fact, to work. So each human has to balance these relationships and for all these complexities, by and large, most of them are perfectly ok.'

'So it's not,' said Stopper, who all the time was thinking that Zero was actually talking about their relationship,' that different from the extended empathetic proximity system is it?'

'No, Stopper, as I said before, they're quite alike.'

'Proximity because they like being with those they like, empathy because they like them, what about extended?'

'Well, their friends have other friends; their lovers have other friends; so it extends as well.'

'You say that one-sided relationships are unhealthy, could that explain the attitude of the capitals?'

'D, d, d, dendrite tree, Stopper, you may be on to something there! Yes, they have a dominance delusion. They think they're dominant but they are not, they are privileged, and there's a difference, their position at the start of a sentence is inherited.'

'They contribute nothing, nothing personal, to meaning either.'

'Yes, we threw that at them once and they argued that meaning was beneath them, which I actually admired for its' panache despite its' ridiculousness. You know, Stopper, we don't actually contribute that much to meaning ourselves do we?'

'That's bollocks, without you Zero the numbers wouldn't sing.'

'That's true enough, and you hold the semantic thread, it's you that pulls it tight in the end.'

'Bloody right, they may look down on us Zero, but it's only to admire the view.'

'Well, Stopper, on that note I think we need, nay, deserve, another drink, if you would take care of that little task I will off to the loo to freshen up. Then we shall resume your manipulation.'

Stopper and Zero were back at their table, manipulations resumed.

'So you know now how the **e**s were able to spread their influence through sheer ubiquity and the commas because they are such damned good hoppers. You also now know that this is still going on in the outside world beyond the confines of this closed circle of lies and well beyond this booth.'

When she said 'booth' Stopper was even more sure that she was still talking about them, though had he selected 'well beyond this booth', he could have held to the same conclusion but would, in fact, have been far closer to the truth.

'There is one other way that language centres communicate with each other, but this only occurs between very close friendships but more often still in long lasting loving couples. Now all language centres use the same letters and punctuations and numbers, which accounts for how they communicate verbally, but each language centre, is unique to each human and the difference between them is akin to a different font. Now in the case of these long term relationships, if in each other's company they find themselves stimulated, that they can reach levels of communication higher than normal then something wonderful happens when a letter in one partner resonates with its counterpart in the other partner and suddenly they flip fonts. This is the sign of a deep meaningful relationship and it has been known for partners to have up to thirty-three percent font exchanges. At that level of interchange the couples have an ease between each other beyond compare. Unfortunately this can have a downside.'

'Now how did I know that was on the way?' Stopper interjected.

'Loss is the downside. Relationship severance comes in three ways, temporal, spatial and permanent. The first type of severance depends on how long the parting lasts. The second type depends on how far apart they are, and how often they can reasonably keep in touch. The third, for obvious reasons, is the worst.'

Stopper, who still thought Zero was talking about their selves, felt sad that after tomorrow night he and Zero would never be together again. Zero though was now thinking this way herself, though she also knew she was describing the plight of the humans, slow, but sure, the gravity of their own situation, forced both of them to think, each, of the other, but the other for each, was not the same.

'So does this 'loss' stuff account for this feeling of alienation that, by all accounts, is a fairly prevalent feeling amongst the humans, in the west at least?'

'No', Stopper, 'the feeling of alienation comes from the social structure imposed on them by the so-called leaders and the cult of the individual that's been imposed on them for the last half-century. It's the artificial constraints that have been put on them that lead to the feeling of alienation. The font exchange, the peer sharing, these are all natural attributes.

'Now when they suffer relationship severance, of whichever type, what happens is that they lose proximity, retain empathy, and the extended joins with the proximity, or you could say that whilst empathy is retained the other two terms are somewhat stretched beyond their semantic perimeters. In both the temporal and spatial severances the font exchange means that even though apart each partner retains a bit of their partner inside and so empathy is retained and proximity gets back into its semantic perimeter. In time, of course full proximity must be achieved in order to satisfy all three semantic containers or words.

'Permanent severance though, is something else again. Where in the temporal and spatial severances the font exchange allows proximity to remain within its' semantic perimeter thereby helping to hold the essence of the relationship together despite the fact that physically they are apart, in permanent severance, the font exchange becomes a curse. The inherent promise of renewed proximity is empty now. The extended part is stretched beyond breaking point, whilst empathy lacking both extension and proximity becomes anguish.'

'Zero', Stopper said quietly, 'I think another drink is called for now.'

"Yes', replied Zero, shaking herself out of her intense reverie, 'You can take care of it?'

'Sure, be back in a bit.'

Phew, thought Stopper on the way to the bar, intense or what, the waves of anguish coming from Zero were palpable now and Stopper at last was realising that she was not just talking about herself and Stopper. Zero had a capacity way beyond her nominal value, and this level of anguish coming from Zero was beyond their selves: her anguish reaching well beyond these limits. Yet even as Stopper was thinking this, Zero, who had been thinking the same way, was in fact now only thinking of herself and Stopper. It was as if there were two sinusoidal waves of empathy out of sync by 90 degrees. Three dimensionally like DNA, and right now, Zero and Stopper were like the seeds of life itself, for just like DNA they would have to unzip each from the other before the next step could be taken, but that time had not yet come, not quite. There were drinks to drink, talk to talk, bills to pay, love to love, and a full day to go. Stopper brought the drinks back to the table.

'The permanent severance, even without the font exchange, is extremely painful for them to go through, but, with the font exchange it's triply painful. On top of the sheer devastation involved in the loss of a partner, the space left where once one had been, the survivors fonts can no longer resonate with the exchanged fonts akin to themselves that were there in the partner, the partner being gone. Also, the bit of the partners self that exchanged with the partner that's gone is no longer close, proximity gone, so the survivor has lost a bit of his or her self.

'So, the survivor has to cope with two losses of selfdom and cope with an increasing realisation of diminished selfdom and these opposing forces feed, each, on the other, in an almost, sometimes too much altogether, unbearable sense of anguish due both to the double loss of the others and the self, which can lead to the survivors becoming, in effect, ghosts of themselves.'

'How do you define ghost?'

'A ghost is an entity that cannot, of its' own volition, reach beyond itself.'

'Hmm, of their own volition...so, when they reach this stage of grief, they are locked into themselves?'

'Yes, well actually, they are locked into their lesser selves.'

'Hmm.'

'You got something Stopper?'

'Yes, possibly, but let's get this finished, there's a lot to take in, we'll come back to this, ok?'

Zero looked over to Stopper more than a little mournfully. 'Yes, I know love, but we've got to finish this, anyway, isn't it usually you remonstrating with me? So they're locked into their lesser selves, unable to reach beyond?'

'Yes,' Zero sighed, 'they're locked in at a low level they can't break out of, there may be friends and family around that sympathise with them and they may be trying their utmost to pull them back from this crippling grief, but sympathy doesn't cut the mustard, only empathy does the job here. To empathise is to get to the same level as the one you wish to connect with, that is, empathy is a purely horizontal connection, whereas sympathy retains some verticality. The empathisers must be whole, complete, undiminished selves, and they must be strong enough to pull them back without succumbing themselves, young children are particularly adept at this, being somewhat more aware of ghosts in the first place, as children are, helps, and they are strong enough by virtue of their opening up life dynamic. Older long time friends can do it but it's very dangerous for them, potentially catastrophic.'

'How so?'

'Older friends may themselves have font exchanges with the survivor, possibly even the deceased, so they may be partly down to their level in the first place, but, not only may they not have the power to pull them back, they may not have the power to pull themselves back.'

'Friendly ghosts.'

'Seeing', Stopper', said Zero, slightly annoyed at having to tangentalise, as it were, her discourse, 'as how friendship, indeed any relationship, demands that each side gets beyond themselves as a precondition for the relationship to exist, then ghosts, by definition, cannot be friendly.'

"So,' did you just get beyond yourself there, or not, he thought, 'they don't all get back?'

'No, most do, but some don't.'

'So what happens to them?'

'They become as ghosts themselves and as ghosts do, they also just fade away, being unable to reach beyond themselves, they can't sustain their perimeters, and consequently, they simply shrink and finally fade away.'

'They always fade away?'

'No, not always, not always Stopper.' Zero fell quiet.

'So what happens when they don't fade away, they stay?'

'They stay, sure they stay, but, linger is probably a better description, they spend the rest of their time trying to figure out why they stayed, so they try and get doing things to justify their staying, but they never complete anything, oh they always say that at least they are travelling hopefully, but you'll always find them at the back of the boat looking back and wondering, and imagining even as they are doing it that at last they are moving forward, and, in a sense they are, but all of it is to avoid the present, the now, the moment...that's where they cannot stay.'

'Do any of them ever come back?'

'No, not that we know of, at least not that we know of yet.'

'There's maybe someone coming back?'

'Maybe, hope so, but then again that someone isn't really gone, but...'

'Someone we know?'

'No, not really...but we may do, we may do.'

'Getting mighty mysterious there my innumerable one.'

'Well of course Stopper, I am the manipulative one am I not?'

'Yeah well sorry about that, wasn't sure what the hell was going on, still no idea really, just got a bit paranoid I guess.'

'No need to apologise, you have been generally right most of the time anyway.'

'Yeah, generally right within the sphere of what I know, but once beyond, it seems that simple ideas start to warp a bit, then a bit more, like the more you get to know the more opaque things get, but I don't know if that is truth or manipulation or some crazy mix of both?'

'Yep, generally right, time to go Stopper, Ed's clearing up, you coming back or you got things to do?'

'Things to do, will try and get back soon, but if not will call round tomorrow, see you soon.'

Zero and Stopper hugged, kissed, and parted as each of them went their separate ways, one headed on towards Oblivion Street that led her home to the starlit dark side of town, whilst the other headed toward the End Times where he was supposed to meet with some emissaries from the Syntactic Street off of Heartbeat Avenue.

As Stopper approached the End Times he saw the number 8 awaiting him outside the tick and talk shop which was a service for letters and punctuation marks having hard times as many characters were having at this period. Inside Stopper met with '*u*' again, 8 of course, the numbers 3 and 2 and letters '**i**' and 's' and '**g**' who were all seated waiting for him.

Although Stopper was finding plenty of evidence pointing towards the capitals being the main party leading to the break-up of the extended empathetic proximity system with all the consequent problems for the letters, numbers and punctuation marks, there had been more than a few reports coming back to him that suggested that numbers were more than a little involved in many of the more recent decisions of the capitals, so Stopper was here to have a discussion with these five to see if he could tease any leading information from any of them.

What concerned Stopper was, that for the numbers to be involved would not be terribly surprising, but he had heard some say that it was the numbers who had instigated the whole attack on the extended empathetic proximity system. Now, Stopper could understand where the Capitals could instigate such a thing given their attitude, arrogance, ignorance, and selfishness coupled with the fact that they were used to starting things without much caring for how they turned out. After all when did you ever see a capital in a word at the beginning of a sentence being affected by the fact that the word is deemed unsuccessful or tainted in some way? The blame may well be directed at the letters within the word, or the semantic direction of the word, or even the way the word somehow doesn't fit into the sentence properly, ironically a situation that disrupts the extended empathetic proximity system, but never is blame diverted in the direction of the capital. The capital just stands aloof, uncaring, and supremely unconcerned. So the capitals were still his prime, though prime he realised was of particular relevance to numbers, targets as it were.

The numbers though didn't seem to have starting things out as a natural instinct kind of thing in themselves really, they were in fact most like the adjectives in the words and letters families in that when coupled with words they lent what was in essence description. 4 oranges, as a phrase, doesn't change the nature of the orange, it multiplies it but it doesn't alter it, and this is most like the way that adjectives work. Adjectives by and large quietly qualify their subjects without subtracting from the quality of the subject in the first place. Indeed it could be said that they add to the quality of the referent, not unlike numbers add. So, no, Stopper knew of no reason to suspect the numbers of instigating anything, but he did think, well actually he knew, it being common knowledge, that numbers and capitals were bosom friends, the capitals feeling, rightly so as it happens being vastly outnumbered by their lower case counterparts, they needed to be close to the numbers in order to use them to their own ends. As far as Stopper knew though the numbers didn't seem to have any designs of their own as regards ambition as such and appeared to be content to enumerate whatever subject counted at that moment. It may well be that had

Stopper read the previous sentence prior to the meeting about to be described, then many of the following sentences describing the ensuing events would in fact not have been written at all but then that could be viewed as part of the very nature of writing itself, if only it did write itself.

'Well my literate and numerate friends I'm most pleased to welcome you to this meeting and I hope I can convince you to help with the punctuation party organisation, but whatever, I am sure that however things end here that there will be adequate contribution from each number of you and each of you who is a number, not to mention a letter.'

'I was beginning to wonder if that 'not to mention line was going to be mentioned at all.' '*u*' said somewhat huffily.

'I couldn't ignore '*u*' now could I, or '**g**' or'**s**' or '**i**' for that matter, though they didn't feel the need to comment on it at all.'

'We did consider,' said g, 'but '*u*' got in first as usual,'

'Yes he does seem to be quick off the mark these days,' '**s**' chipped in,

'He seems to have gotten that way ever since beginning his association with you in fact.' '**m**' concluded.

'Yes,' '**i**' said quietly, it does appear that '*u*' does spend much of his current time chasing full stops as it were.'

'Just the one,' said Stopper, puzzled at why **i** seemed to start in some surprise when he said this, so, for good measure he repeated it once more, 'just the one.' There was no reaction from **i** this time Stopper noticed, once bitten twice shy maybe, he thought, but he lost the thought as it didn't appear to lead anywhere and the conversation begun properly before the thought could find a way out of its own neural undergrowth.

'So, what is it you want us to do Stopper, as regards the punctuation party?' 8 asked.

I'm really just looking for ideas and I thought that you could help with your breadth of experience and maybe give me some pointers to help make the punctuation party successful.'

'Well, you could start,' 2 chipped in, 'by apologising to cap C and thereby stopping, that is something you are supposed to be good at as I recall, the pullout of the capitals from the whole affair.'

This was expected from the numbers for sure but s and g were remarkably quick in offering their support for this apology and although Stopper was initially surprised at their alacrity he did realise that many of the lower case letters were appalled at his accusations against C, and not all of them were turncoats. What did surprise him was the rather lame support they got from 'i'. Indeed the numbers were more forthcoming with their support than 'i'. On top of this after what '*u*' had told him about outsourcing and the like, it was highly unlikely that any capitals were going to be coming to the punctuating party anyway, at least not in person, virtual virtuals in fact, and what were those Stopper thought, his tangential half thought pulling him again, but this was not the place or time.

'Well ok I will apologise for the way I attacked him.'

'That's not a real apology, it's not apologising for the accusation.'

'Well that's as far as I'm prepared to go.' Stopper thought why bother with a real apology when the capitals aren't really going to be there in the first place, or was that second place come to think of it.

Stopper expected '*u*' to back him up, but to his, and '*u*''s, surprise, '**i**' agreed that Stopper was right to apologise in the way he intended, and that any full apology should be given when cap C was fully exonerated.

'Are you saying Stopper was right to throw these, these insults at the cap?' 3 steamed.

'No, no, but as Stopper said at the time, the narrative wasn't right so it is right to wait until the narrative gets straightened out as it were,' said '**i**'.

'Straightened out, sounds positively twisted to me!' said 8.

'That's neat coming from you m8' said '**g**'.

'Now, shouldn't we all calm down a bit,' said '*u*', 'no need for things to get nasty.'

'Hey '*u*',' 8 retorted, 'how come you're always at the back of the q?'

A trio of commas at the bar bust out giggling.

Stopper smiled at this but did ask for a little more respect between the letters and the numbers even if not each for the other, then at least for him and the commas, who immediately giggled again on being mentioned, as the only punctuation marks in the place, it would be better if they didn't feel out of place, at which point the commas giggled again. Stopper reasoned that the commas could be of some help here, at least insofar as slowing things down a bit, so he asked them to join them, which, after a customary, or so it would seem, giggle, they did.

So, the commas seated themselves between '*u*', '**s**', and '**g**', and joined the company which seemed to temper their somewhat unlettered behaviour they had so far been enjoined in. Once they were settled in *u* said, 'Maybe now some of us might find a way to get a word in edgeways.'

'Let's see if we can get some words out front ways '*u*'.'

'Well,' said the number 3, 'maybe we can enumerate some points, just to help us organise our thoughts.'

'Fair enough,' Stopper said, 'let's see: entertainment, safety, security, publicity and support. That ought to help you focus.'

'Well,' 8 volunteered with some enthusiasm, 'If you need someone to handle entertainment Stopper, there is none here more qualified or experienced or, for that matter, willing.'

'**s**', being elbowed with some force by a comma, spoke up, 'You can count me in on that one too.' he said somewhat breathlessly.

'Steady on,' said '*u*', 'we can't have everyone in entertainment, now can we?'

'Why not?' '**s**' replied, 'if everyone is entertained they aren't going to worry too much about everything else are they, let's put on a show!'

'We can't just ignore safety and security not to mention support, now can we?'

'They will, give them some food and drink, entertain them, and they won't care a whit about anything else.'

The commas, always prone to entertainment scenarios, voiced their support for this idea in full triple chorus. The numbers weren't too sure about this though, feeling that safety and security should be paramount, minimum requirement one of them argued, to allow the entertainment to flourish. The letters fell on both sides of the argument as they were prone to do and Stopper, who was struggling to make any sense of anything out of this, was becoming concerned over the relative unconcern for security given the events of the last punctuation party.

'We can't ignore security,' said Stopper, 'especially after what happened last time, after all no one has seen Halter or Hold since.'

'Well that was a magic trick wasn't it, to make them disappear. I remember everyone applauded; spectacular stuff.'

'Yes, wasn't it just, but as I recall the point of a disappearing act is to make the disappeared reappear, as if by magic, but the reappearance didn't, in fact, reappear, indeed you could argue that the reappearance itself disappeared without a trace along with Halter and Hold.'

'Bloody hell Stopper, they were pissed, they were completely full, full stops, probably couldn't find their way back,'

'For a year, are you kidding me?'

'Maybe they took a sabbatical?'

'Sabbatical: when the hell did those start? Syntax sakes I want one now! Delay that sentence, Stoppers is on leave!'

'It was magic at the time,' one of the commas chimed in, 'but not when they didn't come back.'

'That's right,' the second comma said, 'we got on well with Halter and Hold, we miss them.'

'I preferred Hold myself.'

'Yes, we can remember your partiality my dear.'

'Now hold on...'

'I believe that was the very terminology.'

The comma with the 'partiality' to Hold looked distressed as the other two commas rounded on her. Stopper stepped in, as it were, saying, 'Now I think we've had enough of your period romances for now.'

'You always stop our fun Stopper.'

'It's my job my dear, my job. Now, can we get back on the subject?'

'Whose subject would that be, we had a subject, at least one of us did as I recall, who says you always get to pick the subject anyway?'

Stopper who was about to argue for the hindsight talent, conveniently forgetting Zeros description of it as a fallacy was interrupted in his intent by the numbers who suggested that subjects are subject to objection and demotion by subsequent sentence reappraisal. This appraisal, they added, was of course under the purview of Stopper but there being more commas than full stops here then the sentence momentum would likely be on the commas side, at least until the end of the sentence.

Sidling up to Stopper '*u*' said 'This sounds like painting by numbers kind of thing.'

'Yes, but then numbers are not known for their eloquence, it would appear that majority rules is their target.' Stopper replied quietly to '*u*'. To the rest of the company he said, 'Well when you consider that the commas and I were discussing Halter and Hold, both full stops as it happens, then that makes three commas and three full stops which would appear to be a complete balance between momentum and reappraisal.'

'Now, that sounds like a full stop.' '**g**' said.

'Exactly,' said Stopper, 'now what did you say about reappraisal?'

'Now, hold on a minute,' said '**i**', 'you say three full stops and three commas? Well, I can see three commas and one full stop, not three, and that gives momentum the edge.'

'You can't see three; guess you're not on the same page as us then eh?'

'Smart Stopper but they are not here!'

'Neither, '**i**', are we, when you get right down to it, we're virtuals after all.'

'What's that, virtuals, us?' 3 cried, 'Good sentence Stopper, what are you trying to say?'

'We're all virtuals,' Stopper said, 'what's the problem?'

'Virtuals: us? Why, we're as real as you Stopper!' The commas cried.

'Well of course you are,' Stopper replied.

'See, there you go, we're as real as Stopper, now what's wrong with that?'

'Are we really virtual?' asked '**u**'.

'Well yes, though you could put it the other way around and say that we're virtually real.'

'What's the difference?'

'Not too sure myself, to tell the truth, though from what I've recently learned is that it would appear that any self reflecting entity is in practise virtual, even though the entity is real.'

'What does that mean?'

'It means, Stopper paused, and then continued, 'Hell, I don't really know. It seemed right when I said it.'

'Oh well, maybe you were virtually right.'

'Actually, Zero once told me that imagination lifted off from reality but it didn't always get back.'

'Well, imagine that eh,' interrupted 'i', 'we're not real, but we're virtually real, and possibly really virtual, but being imagined we're beyond reality and we don't have to go back.'

'I'm not altogether sure that that is the right way to look at it.'

'You look at it your way,' said 'i', 'and I'll look at it mine.'

'Yes, well of that I have no doubt, after all any sentence is open to interpretation, after I've done my bit that is.'

'It's amazing the changes in interpretation you can suggest with a well placed s and a carefully put apostrophe,' suggested 's' in a most suggestive way.

'That I know, courtesy of a pair of inverted commas.'

'Have you been speaking to our cousins Stopper?' asked the commas, 'Did you get any good quotes?'

'Yes we had a very interesting discussion, some of which may well have been quotable, but nothing trips off the lips right now as it were.'

'Well,' said number 3, 'nice imaginative romp, but it's time to get back to reality, now who is going to handle the food and refreshments, and the little things for pleasure?'

'That just has to be my job, Stopper; I'm a dab hand at refreshments.' 8 said.

'No 8, I think you will be the main number for entertainment, seeing as that's your forte, I thought maybe 3 would look after the refreshments, he doesn't look as full as you so he could have a few nibbles on the side, but from you we want your musical offerings.'

'What about security then?' asked '**g**'.

'He who asks gets.' Stopper replied, 'The job is yours, and i's too and s can look after safety if that's ok with everyone and we can all of us can go and think about the tasks to hand and finalise our arrangements at the semantic club and deal with the details then.'

Everyone agreed to this and after a brief talk amongst themselves they then got up and left the building. They stayed together to cross the road outside when they were beckoned down this alleyway by a first bracket ushering them along. Suddenly the very ground beneath them shook and gave way, like some kind of brainquake, the commas screamed in panic, '***u***' became almost upright in his efforts to keep himself upright, '**g**' was upended, '**s**' slid to the floor, just before it disappeared, then the numbers also disappeared, as if by magic, and all of them, except the disappeared numbers, tumbled down into darkness.

END OF PART ONE

First Interlude

'Stopper, you there,' cried '*u*' in the dark, 'what happened, where are we? Is everyone here?'

Stopper could hear various others groan and mutter in the darkness and quietly said 'Hold on a minute till I get some perspective here.'

'How do you get perspective in the pitch dark Stopper', one of the commas said.

A soft glow began to emanate from the darkness and slowly they began to make each other and their surroundings out. It was '**g**' who first noticed that the glow was coming from Stopper himself and asked how he did that.

'As a full stop I have hindsight, the satisfaction of completion, and when needs must, as now, the soft glow of understanding.' Stopper replied.

'So, where are we, anyone any idea?' asked '**s**'.

'We appear to be in the unconscious if my least wild guess is correct' said '*u*'.

'Indeed we are my friend, indeed we are, but whose is the question, whose?' Stopper said.

'Does it matter,' asked '**i**', surely all we need to know is how to get out of here and as you seem to be the purveyor of a soft light of understanding surely you can lead the way.'

'As regards whose unconscious,' Stopper replied, 'it doesn't much matter, one is much the same as any other when you get right down to it as we seem to have done. It does matter whose unconscious it is as regards the subconscious that we eventually get back to, what kind of society it has and what characters are there.'

'There might be more full stops there Stopper.' A comma suggested.

'You're just hoping to find Hold here,' said another.

'I am not.' She protested.

'Oh yes you are.' Another said. 'Oh yes you are.'

'Well, whatever unconscious we are in, I don't think we're here completely by chance and I don't think we're here just to go straight into the subconscious, we're here for a reason and I intend to find out what it is.' Stopper said.

The commas were nervous; letters 's' and 'g' were, if anything, even more nervous, whilst the letter 'i' was trying to insist that they go straight back whence they came. Stopper pointed out that they didn't actually know how to get back whence they came, come to that they didn't know how to get wherever they were meant to go and they didn't know how to get to the subconscious awaiting them. Furthermore, Stopper being the bearer of the only light in the company meant wherever he chose to go all had to go. So for once rather than a full stop following all the letters, words and punctuation marks, the full stop was leading the way forward to somewhere as yet unknown. Whilst to the 'i', they were very much travelling the wrong way. No-one payed him much attention though other than two of the commas remarking that it was not like lower case 'i' to call so much attention to himself, and that if he kept up like this and Stopper wandered off, he could be mistaken by his constant self attention of being a capital in the dark as it were. The letter i became quieter after overhearing that.

The first thing was to take in their immediate environment and try and get some kind of bearings as to which direction to take. As they looked around, it was only as each of them spotted each other that they fully realised how their own faces were distorted in distaste by the expressions of their mutual perceptions and then their extended realisations that this was not an environment that was suitable for the likes of them at all. No letters or punctuation marks had been in this kind of place before.

There were no flat surfaces here, everything was kind of tubular and curved, the surface they stood upon was of a convoluted appearance, it gave way a little like a sponge, though no moisture seemed to be squeezed out. There was no noise, and even their own voices seemed to struggle to be heard here, all sound fell dead and was sucked into the sponge-like surfaces never to be heard again. It was not an area that assisted vocal communication at all and but for Stoppers soft light, visibility was not highlighted either. Here were no straight lines to speak of, no pathway was evident and overall there was no feel of welcome here at all.

Into this, Stopper, possessing neither hindsight, nor eyesight to speak of, and only wishing for foresight, toiled to lead his lost letters and literary speed bumps who were for all intents and purposes useless, clueless, and meaningless in an environment without any support systems for their kind. Stopper himself knew that the longer they were here, the less they would be able to cope, and beyond some indeterminate and undoubtedly short time they simply would not survive. Yet Stopper could not reveal this to his companions, and he hoped that they would not come to this conclusion themselves for there is no sadder fate for letters than a sentence of inexistence.

There was a dark and brooding silence as they trudged through this featureless brainscape and it being difficult to speak they fell into a forlorn silence broken only by the quiet sighs of the commas as they tripped over the convoluted surfaces. Then the silence that was slowly oppressing their very sense of language was split by a horrendous scream that made the entire brain area tremble, waves of invisible anguish washed over everything and all of them quailed and cowered in abject fear. Fear was the only sense left them, hope was despair, the commas held close to each other, letters were hugged by one another, none knew quite why, but it was probably for empathetic proximity as well as comfort, but nothing was extended here other than neurons.

The scream came again even louder as if closer, were they still moving, they weren't sure, but if they hadn't moved then the scream had and that was not an encouraging thought. Stopper assured them that they were still moving and that they were approaching the source of the scream and that he did not really know why but that somehow he knew that they had to get through this scream in order to get back to their subconscious. The letters already looking doubtful looked doubly doubtful at this, whilst the commas simply nodded their acquiescence to their already miserable situation.

The scream tore through them again, distorting the letters out of shape, and sending the commas flying backwards tail over tail. They were close now; Stopper said he thought it was just round this corner, though the concept of corner was somewhat difficult to conceive of in this convoluted cauliflower that was itself the cauldron of mental conception. They went round the bend to find the source of the scream right in front of them as it cleared its' throat for another banshee roar: they were directly facing the fearsome figure of the Amygdala!

No letter or punctuation mark, italicised or not, had ever heard anything like that scream, some, as they barely endured it, thought that this was the last sound they were ever going to hear, whilst almost all the letters were distorted almost beyond recognition, only Stopper was relatively unaffected, being of a completely rounded contour, the force emitted from the scream of the Amygdala had nothing to push on in any direction in favour of any other, so he had a little time to observe the particular distortions of the letters that had landed in this place with him. The scream, seemingly endless, ended, and under cover of the last of its effect the Amygdala quietly said, 'Welcome Stopper. I've been waiting for you.'

'So,' Stopper said, nodding to his companion's phantasmagorical distorted shapes slowly morphing into something resembling themselves, 'I heard.'

Phantasmagorical might not at first read seem to be the appropriate adjective but the light in this area was no longer the soft understanding light of Stopper. There was a baleful light in this place, with an almost greenish tinge, there was no reflection here. The walls, for want of a better word, and believe you me a better word was wanted, seemed to suck what light there was into itself, this was a light that not only did not reflect or refract; the light itself simply oozed fear; this was a light that cast no shadow; it contained its own.

At least that awful scream had stopped and although the ensuing silence was a relief, for the briefest of times, this noiselessness became almost palpable in its seeming sponge-like ability to absorb even the slightest hint of sound, words here barely held together for their own duration, fading quietly into the next one with barely any gap as if this noiselessness sucked silence itself out of play. The commas chattered rapidly amongst themselves to try and keep this baleful, awful, vacuous emptiness at bay. The individual letters were beginning to fray, to lose their fontness; their definition as particular letters was under threat. All they could do was try and hold themselves together as individual letters, there not being enough of them to make a word, not that that would have helped much here anyway. Here, in the depths of the unconscious, was an absolute reality with no support for anything else. The scene may well have been the stuff of nightmares but this was no place for the imagination.

'Do you have to scream like that?' asked Stopper.

'Certainly I do, it's my job.' Replied the Amygdala

'It's your job to generate fear?'

'It is indeed, anyway, I'm only the broadcaster, the news is gathered from elsewhere, and from what I've been told there's a lot out there to be scared of.'

'You don't think that maybe you kind of overstate it?'

'No, Stopper, I only react to the information I receive.'

'What if the information is wrong?'

'That's not my concern Stopper, I'm here to broadcast alarms, I mean, sure we might get false information sometimes but well, worst case scenario, better safe than sorry, if it wasn't for me and all that, well it is largely true. The hosts, Stopper, may well be much safer than they used to be when worry was just about all they knew, but they are still surrounded by potential dangers, both inside and out, half of which is why you are here Stopper.'

'Yes, I can guess which half too, but isn't it a case that the problem here does seem to be a case of too much misinformation?'

'Well, there's really no such thing as misinformation in the unconscious Stopper, just straight chemical potentials really and down here chemical potentials always tell the truth, the trouble would appear to be in the translation as it were.'

'The translation,' asked Stopper, 'from where?'

'From the conscious host by all accounts.'

'I thought there was no meaningful communication from the consciousness to the unconscious?'

'There isn't really, but the subconscious can and often does alter the flow of the chemical potentials and thereby influence things here and by effect up there. Anyway there's something badly wrong up there Stopper, I've been screaming till I'm hoarse, don't get me wrong, I like my job, but there are limits. So you have to find out what the problem is, and what's causing it, but for now you can't go back into the subconscious you came from, that's been closed off now, and you can't go up into the main one because of the problems you have to find out about, so you have to go up into another one on the far right. You'll emerge on the right side of the brain, that's where you should be, that's where to start looking. Oh, there's a message for you here, Stopper, here you go.'

'There's nothing written here', Stopper said.

'There is, but all we had was a few spare chemicals which turned out to have the same quality as invisible ink.'

'Can't you remember what it was?'

'Remember? Got no call for memory round here, visit the cortex or the hippocampus if you want memory cells. Anyway, you'd better get going Stopper, your friends are looking a bit worse for wear and if they stay much longer they'll look like invisible ink themselves.'

'So how do you carry out this conversation if you've no memory?'

'Oh that's easy, subconscious flow of chemical potentials, Speediflow they call it I believe, it's not really me you're talking to, Hell Stopper,' he interrupted his talk to release a long scream, 'I wouldn't have the time.' and resumed his screaming.

'Stopper, where have you been?' The commas screamed at the top of their voices to compete with the screams of the Amygdala. Stopper looked around and saw that the letters he had left behind were almost completely fontless now, at least in any recognisable form that is. The italicised '*u*' was actually in a somewhat better state than the others because he had angled his *u*ness in such a way as to have the main force of the scream to wash around him and not fill his cup, the '**g**' had angled his self to resemble a pair of discarded spectacles, whilst the '**s**' had writhed around some before settling down as a scribble. Stopper looked at the' '**i**, and saw that like the '*u*' , he too had angled himself to let the force of the scream wash over him, but in doing that he almost lost his hat, so he angled himself into the wind of the Amygdala to save his hat, though Stopper looking from a certain angle could have sworn he was wearing a toupee, the vanity of that 'i'!

'I've been talking to the Amygdala.' Stopper replied. The commas, who were always chasing Stopper for advice on the nature of pauses almost straightened out in consternation, '***u***' nearly straightened up himself, whilst '**s**', after scribbling a quick note to himself, slid across the undulating floor to get a better view, finally g, doing his best not to make a spectacle of himself said, 'Stopper, you could not have been speaking to the Amygdala, he never stopped screaming.'

'Well, yes you're right of course, but I was talking with the subconscious through the Amygdala and there's a few problems we have to find out about and then to sort out.'

'A few problems, you are telling me! What are you talking about Stopper; I don't think you were talking with anyone, or anything for that matter.'

'What do you mean I wasn't talking, look I've got a message.'

'Stopper, there's nothing written here.'

'Yes there is,' cried Stopper triumphantly, 'it's written in invisible ink!'

'Yeah, right,' said '**i**', 'what do we do, guess what it says?'

'Invisible ink, Stopper, you been on the chemicals again?' asked '***u***'.

'Nothing stronger than ink,' Stopper replied

'Would that be invisible ink,' asked '**g**', 'taken clandestinely no doubt.'

'We believe what you're saying Stopper, were just not sure what you are saying, but we think we can sort that all out later.' The commas piped up in support of a clearly weakened Stopper.

Stopper, whilst noticing the detrimental conditions of his companions had not noticed or even considered his own condition and had no idea at all that his full stopness was disintegrating into blobness. In the meantime s was missing his hastily scribbled note and none of them had fully realised that they were well away from the Amygdala and that they had all been moving for some time. Stopper told them that they were unable to remember things because there was no call for memory down here, which was why 's' had lost his note and none of them could remember getting there. 'g', who had become the most vociferous critic of Stopper in his weakened state said he had misheard what Stopper had just said and that it would be appreciated if he could repeat it for his sake. Stopper looked at 'g' for what may have been a long time, but maybe it wasn't that long, he could never remember, which is what he said to 'g' there and then; 'I can't remember.'

It appeared that 'g' and 'i' were teaming up to attack a clearly weak Stopper when '𝑢' cried out that there was an end bracket up ahead and all previous animosity was completely forgotten as they exultantly made their way to the final bracket of the unconscious to re emerge in a very different subconscious from what they had previously known.)

PART TWO

Stopper and his companions were taken to the font repair and ink transfusion hospital where they were all touched up nicely before being shown into an office where some officious looking capitals in severe angular fonts were waiting to ask them some officious questions in what turned out to be a beyond the bracket investigation.

The capitals were asking Stopper why they had gone beyond the bracket in the first place, what had happened there, where they'd gone, where they'd come from, and what they'd come back this way for.

Stopper told them that they hadn't actually seen the open bracket until they were past it by which time it was too late and that after that they'd had no choice but to seek for the closed bracket which they had in fact done. As regards the time in between the brackets, Stopper said that he had no memory of that time, that in fact there was little call for memory in there as it was possibly a fully complete semantic aside, with no influence and no memory. They then asked Stopper what words preceded him and Stopper told them that unfortunately he had only the company of a few letters and commas, not near enough for words or sentences to clarify events between the brackets, and anyway, he suggested that with no memory there would not have been much use for them, that all they could have done under those circumstances was to create a few cross words, which may have provided a few clues to some, but would have been a waste of space to others. They quizzed Stopper a little longer but gave up when they realised that they were wasting their time. They spent a little more time with the other letters and even less time with the commas, capitals rarely having any contact with commas meant that that particular interview was awkward to say the least, for the capitals that is, for the commas came out giggling at the end of it anyway.

Stopper was waiting for everyone to gather round again, he particularly wanted to speak to the s once they were beyond the confines of this place. Looking around, he saw the number 1 speaking to some capitals which was nothing unusual as the numbers and the capitals were often seen together, he looked at the company to see who was missing and spotted the 'i' coming in to join them which seemed to be all of them back together again, looking back to the capitals he was looking at before he saw that they were looking their way but the number 1 was nowhere to be seen now, and whatever his business there was, it would appear, to have been concluded. Anyway, he thought, it's no business of ours. As they were all together again Stopper suggested they find some place to relax and try and make some sense of where they'd been, where they were, and where, hopefully, they were going.

As they began to look for some place to sit and talk they began to realise that this was a very different place from the previous subconscious they'd come from, very different indeed. In the old place there were no shortage of cafes and although the streets were a bit unkempt and there were many unlit streets and dark areas where few would ever go, they'd all kind of gotten used to that, but this was definitely a subconscious that served a very different host if ever there was one. This was clean and well lit, streets were straight, indeed they appeared to be organised in a complex geometric arrangement that they couldn't make out from their location. Beyond this structure though darkness reigned supreme, there was no way, they thought, that anyone would want to go there. They finally found a place to go, they served drinks and there were seats but it had none of the warmth they remembered from the likes of whispers and hearsay, but it was a chance to catch up, functional if nothing else.

After settling down Stopper called the 's' over to his side and asked him if he had his note. The 's' said that yes he did and that he had a vague memory of having scribbled on it but that there was nothing on it at all; it was just a sheet of paper. Stopper told the s not to worry about that and after asking the 'u' to fetch over a small candle he asked the 's' if he could do a little pluralisation for him and ask each of the pluralised s's to bring their notes to Stopper. Once the 's' or s's had done their bit, or bits, Stopper had 8 notes altogether and he began to waft these over the flame of the candle. The other letters and commas looked on in some consternation, none of them having any idea what Stopper was doing, but when the shapes of letters began to darken and form from the effect of the heat the letters and commas looked on in awe: magic, said the commas in unison. Stopper repeated the process for each of the 8 notes and put each finished one on top of the last until all of them were done.

'So what is this then Stopper?' Asked 'g'.

'These,' Stopper responded, 'are notes from another subconscious from Zero through the Amygdala.'

'I thought you couldn't remember anything from in there, I couldn't, how could you?'

'I didn't, Zero told me to ask s for his note once we came through the bracketed aside, and she also told me that there were 8 notes and that getting the s to pluralise would enable them to be read.'

'So how'd you know about the flame and stuff then?' asked '**s**'.

'Well there was nothing on the notes but I knew that Zero, even if her name means nothing to you, would in fact not send me nothing and I remembered the story of the Ghost of the Amygdala and the Missing Letter.'

'Never mind that,' said '*u*' 'what's in the notes?'

'Don't you want to hear The Ghost of the Amygdala and the Missing Letter?'

'Oh yes', cried the commas, who could never resist a good story for long, 'Please, please, please.'

'Well,' said Stopper in a conspiratorial manner, 'we were not the first asides to go through the brackets you know.'

'No,' they all, except for '*u*', answered in unison.

'No, there were others who preceded us...'

'Others, other letters?' asked '**s**'.

'Were there any commas?'

A larger group of letters than us, I think if I remember rightly they were enough to make up some words, maybe even a sentence to begin with, but I can't remember which ones.'

'Can you remember which letter was missing? Maybe we can work it out from that?'

'Maybe that's pushing the art of deduction a tad too far, we don't know which letters, words or sentence but we're suppose to work it out from one missing letter, might just about manage an acronym if it wasn't more than three letters.'

'If there was a sentence there could have been punctuation.'

'Was it still a sentence without the missing letter?'

'Does it matter; this is a story about the letters, not by the letters, or even by the letters minus one come to that.'

'Would you get on with it then?'

'Alright, this sentence, for want of a better word to describe the group of letters that followed the wretched path to the Amygdala found themselves at the mercy of the screams and took longer than we did to find their way round and back through the close bracket.'

'They did get back though, yes?' asked the commas, who were excitably eager to hear but had to ask silly questions to quell their eagerness by beckoning an answer that would serve as a relief, and even though they already knew the answer the sense of relief was still there. The sense of anticipation of course would heighten shortly after as the effect of the interruption and the consequent postponement created by it worked their effects through the discourse, this would inevitably lead to yet another rhetorical question from the commas, and on it went.

'Well, of course, they got back, all bar one presumably, or else there wouldn't ever be a tale called The Ghost of the Amygdala and the Missing Letter, now would there?'

'So, yes they got back but as they were treating the tainted fonts and forms of the letters some of them began to ask for one of them who didn't seem to be there and although few took much notice at first they all began to realise that something was wrong before long. The better off of them began to look for the missing letter but no-one knew where it was. He'd last been seen back at the

Amygdala but no-one remembered having spotted him since. A couple of them suggested they go back out to the Amygdala and see if they could find him but the general consensus was that this was going too far, which I am sure you can understand having just been through the experience. I shouldn't think anyone here would relish a return to the Amygdala... no, I thought not. As they guiltily gave up hope they began to resume their lives of letters and for a while things seemed to turn back to normal. As time went on though, as these same surviving letters were asked to come out and play their parts in words and sentences, they were all freelance letters of course, then words kept on appearing with missing letters and not only did it turn out that the words in which the missing letters appeared, or is that not appeared, tricky one that, there were always letters from the trip to the Amygdala and the missing letter was the same letter missing after that trip. As the story got around employment prospects for the 'guilty' letters, for so they were now deemed, became fewer and farther between, though some of them still managed employment in horror stories, maybe even this one, now that would be neat.'

'Yes, I'll have to see if I can get a copy.' '**s**' piped up.

'If you're lucky you should be able to get one free.' said '*u*'.

'Oh yeah, how do you work that out then?' asked 's'.

'If you are the missing letter then you could complete the story.'

'I'll have to think about that one.'

'Well, best think about it after you've heard the rest of the story then eh?'

'In a fairly short while all of the letters that had been with the missing letter were all unemployed, all of them, they never went out, they were shunned in public, no-one called, other than names that is, and here's the strange thing, they began to lose their fontness, their form, oh much slower this time, much slower altogether, just like they had on the trip to the Amygdala.'

'Ooh, spooky' said the commas, 'but what of the missing letter?'

'There had been strange tales of drinks being drunk whilst heads were turned, food being taken whilst attention was elsewhere, some reports of plates of stuff floating off of the table and drinks being upturned to empty into thin air. Everyone had by this time forgotten completely all about the missing letter, and no-one had seen the 'guilty' letters for ages so no-one put two and two together as it were, so all of these tales were put down to too much imagination, drink and merriment taking attentions elsewhere, yet it never really stopped. These incidents kept happening and tales were told and theories were expanded on, but still not enough ever got together to warrant a full investigation. So time went by as it does and apart for the usual kind of things and the odd kind of things everything was the same. Then out on one of the darker streets, it was a little cold that time, no-one knew why, but someone had had the idea of starting a fire, which they promptly did. As the flames rose up and the heat began to spread a ghostly shape began to form nearby, everyone was looking at the flames as most will do, so nobody noticed for a while until a late comer stopped still pointing with his breath held and somehow saying, 'It's missing!', though some say they thought they misheard, as the rest of them pulled themselves free of the spell of the flames. As they turned to see the ghostly form of the missing letter, which was to all intents and purposes asleep and completely unaware of any of this, shimmering peacefully through it all, they all, as one, possibly even as one word, screamed at the sight of this apparition. The apparition then woke to the sound of the screams and feeling the gazes of the others on him, an experience mildly reminiscent, but given the unexpectedness of this situation somewhat enhanced, of The Amygdala experience, he quailed and shimmered and darted away as ghosts apparently are apt to do.

'A new search party was formed, a research party in fact, and as the news spread through the ether, as it were, and as the research party passed by the long closed doors of the long term unemployed 'guilty' letters, curtains twitched in the windows, but no-one saw who peered through the unwashed panes. All of the party carried torches and they split to radiate through the streets that headed out to the darkness. When they got there, they lit up the edge of the darkness, which made the darkness itself retreat, thereby creating a fiery perimeter around the web of streets within. Encouraging others to join in and furnishing them with torches in time the entire web-like arrangement of streets were lit up by what seemed like rivers of fire, the whole place lit up, incandescent, yet still the missing letter was not to be seen. In the streets themselves the doors of the long term unemployed began to open as they were encouraged to join in the search, after all, if the missing letter was found then they could go back to freelance jobbing, though, it must be said, some of them would need complete makeovers at the ink and font clinic to get anywhere near presentable again. Indeed, some of them were so far gone that some others, seeing what appeared to be a torch holding itself aloft, presumed they had found the missing letter. It took some persuasion to correct them of their mistaken identification, to convince them that these letters in fact were the letters that were missing the missing letter and not the missing letter. In fact it was all resolved when one group encountered another group who had both made the same mistake. Once they realised that there couldn't be two of them as there was only one missing letter they made their apologies, with some mitigation pleas for sure, and they all began to research again. In one of the streets a door opened and closed just beyond the light of the flames and two torches floated out, it seemed, on air. These two torches began a slow, halting, journey through the streets toward the centre of the town, and though they were occasionally hailed and stopped as being potentially the missing letter, the fact that there was two of them gave them relatively free passage through the fire lit streets.

'The centre of town was relatively empty at that time as most letters were out seeking their long lost comrade as the two torches made their way to cross the street to the ink and font touch up centre, locally known as the ink well. No-one saw the two torches lean over and dowse themselves releasing a long series of hisses as the flames died and ambient light took over. Soft faltering footfalls made their way to the front desk where a completely unaware secretary, exclamation marks tended to take up these positions, was startled by what appeared to be a disembodied cough somewhere just in front of her. Then, just to startle her even more a disembodied voice began to speak, 'I've brought...' as another joined in to say, 'I am...' and both simultaneously said, 'the missing letter.' In a fusion that resulted in complete confusion which itself resulted in a profusion of voices some disembodied and one, very much in your face. The cacophony of voices began to resemble the oncoming scream of the Amygdala in intensity and hurt. A higher official, a capital came in and having some independence of thought back in those pre-acronymic days realised that they had the missing letter in the ink well. Taking charge he immediately summoned some nurses and demanded that they get what seemed to him to be the missing letter into a ward for immediate treatment. This letter was wheeled away to the ward but unfortunately the other letter, missed in the confusion, in exhaustion sank to the floor.

'As it happened the capital had in fact picked the right letter as far as need for treatment was concerned, if not the correct identification as regards the missing letter, but as the first letter was being brought back from the brink of blankness, the other letter was squirming around spending the last of its fontness and form all over the floor. The secretary who was still lost in confusion trying to figure out how she thought she'd heard another voice but there was no-one there to claim ownership, came out from behind the front desk and promptly tripped up over whatever was down there that she couldn't see. This was simply too much for our highly strung exclamation mark who, beginning to make her own bid for Amygdala like screaming, alerted others, a little more alert due mostly to not being totally freaked out, to this squirming half seen thing on the floor.

'Nurses were summoned to rescue the fading letter but as soon as they tried to pick the letter up to put him on a stretcher, used to get them back to proper font size, they found he simply slipped out of their grasp. This happened time and time again and the entire scene disintegrated into farce in front of everyone else's eyes. What they saw was two question marks bending over and reaching down and straightening up, slowly at first, then a couple of jerks, and then a sudden release and straightening up, and wavering before starting the whole pantomime all over again. Each time would get faster and quickly the question marks would lose their footing until they too ended up on the floor, looking for the kind of questions that give only certain answers by this time. Hyphen delivery was just at that point delivering some ink to the place as one of the question marks lunged for an answer and got in the hyphens way. The hyphen dropped a big bottle of ink which went splat all over the floor and created even more commotion than there had already been. As the melee subsided and one of the question marks got back to her feet she could see that the letter they had been grappling with was in fact the missing letter they had all been looking for, which due to this ink spillage could now be seen and therefore could be dealt with in relative ease. The other question mark got to her feet and brushed herself down and as they bent to finally put the missing letter onto the stretcher, the exclamation mark screeched, 'If that's the missing letter, who was taken in there before?' She was addressing the question marks.'

'Oh, who's the mystery letter?' asked one comma.

'Who's the missing letter then?' asked another.

'All in good time ladies, all in good time, now: as the news spread quickly through the researchers, the flames began to converge on the ink well as the darkness once again encroached upon the edge of town and the flames ran down the streets to leave them behind, the dark air behind the flames were full of questions, mainly how was the missing letter and who was the mystery letter, and the light ahead seemed to promise answers. At the ink well a cordon of hyphens was moved into place to prevent any unwanted incursions that would interfere with the health treatment of the two letters, mystery and missing, I always thought that would be a splendid name for a detective agency myself, or confuse any intelligence gathering occupations in the ink well regarding the stories behind the two letters, mystery and missing, you know it really would be a superb name for a detective agency that.

'The mystery letter, as we mentioned before, was rather worse for wear as he'd been affected badly by long term unemployment, no extended empathetic proximity time for a long time, and no voice, so fontness, visibility and clarity were all damaged badly along with some residual damage from the Amygdala experience that had been missed at the time. In the treatment room where operations were ongoing to make the letter readable again, the letter found the whole experience extremely painful so that during treatment he was always leaning away in a futile attempt to lessen the pain, this gave him a permanent deformity in that the mystery letter is now permanently italicised.'

'It's you,' they all cried looking at '*u*' in a mixture of sympathy, awe and admiration, whilst '*u*', looking even more italicised than usual as if trying to get away from all this attention, said that it was nothing really, just an adventure too far.

'So why, good lines, what in sentences name inspired you to go again?' asked '**g**'.

'Stopper wanted someone with previous experience and being italicised I knew that I could take the scream at a better angle as it were, with far less damage, so I could keep a better eye on the rest of you and on Stopper himself who had to get up close to the Amygdala, which was an extremely dangerous position to get into, though Stoppers roundness and smallness were of great help, he still needed someone there to call if things were going wrong.'

'You mean, if things were going more wrong than they already were, don't you?' asked the commas.

'Well, yes, I expect I am, whatever it's Stopper who is the hero, not me, I'm just glad to help.'

'Well '*u*', Zero always sings your song down at numbers; *I'll always be italicised for you.*' Stopper replied.

'Anyway,' said '*u*', 'what about the missing letter, we've still to get to the rest of the story.'

'Alright, alright, on we go...now, where were we, oh yes, I remember now. They were treating *u* in the treatment room at the ink well, and, as you know now, there is only one, and as we know he wasn't having the best of times when they brought the missing letter for treatment. So, given *u*'s pain and his relative stability by this time, he was moved into a temporary bed whilst they began to treat the missing letter. Outside in the foyer, where the secretary was finally getting herself into a presentable state of mind, the long term post Amygdala unemployed letters, who did not look terribly good themselves were becoming concerned by the fact that they seemed to missing two of their number. Now they knew that one of them was being treated, and they now knew that that was in fact '*u*'. So, who, they wondered was the other missing letter and was the missing letter in the treatment room the missing letter they had all been looking for, or was it the letter they had just recently realised was missing. As they now appeared to have two missing letters they decided that they would split their group into two, one group per missing letter. One group stayed in the treatment centre to hear of '*u*', and the missing letter there, whilst the other group went off to look for the other missing letter elsewhere.

'The streets were empty now after the day's commotions and fires but all was quiet now as the group went off in search of their newly noticed missing letter. As they searched the streets they realised that given their condition and not knowing, but presuming that the missing letter would be in at least as bad a condition as they themselves were and possibly worse, then what were the chances of them just coming across him by chance? One of them suggested that they start the search at the letters address, that maybe he'd never come out of doors during the search at all and having ascertained that the missing letter they were after lived on the street opposite the numbers in between the Tab inn and the letter '**w**', off they went to investigate.

Arriving at the address they could see that it didn't even look lived in, not at least for some time, but given how they themselves had rather left their own surroundings less than desirable, this did not necessarily mean that the letter would not be there. Knocking on the door there was no answer, they didn't expect one, after all, none of them had been in the habit of answering their own doors for some time. Looking in the windows they couldn't see much at first but one of them thought they could see the letter sat on the sofa, but looking strangely still, another had a look and thought that it was just the impression of the letter on the sofa, that the letter itself wasn't there at all. Yet another had a look and decided that the answer was undecidable. Taking a closer look they found that the door wasn't locked, well, to be precise the lock was broken, so unlocked is in use here more a technical term rather than true, but, that aside, they went in. In the deep gloom of the inside as they approached the sofa of the missing letter '**q**' they still found it difficult to tell whether '**q**' was there or not, or it was just an impression. As they neared the sofa they realised with mounting horror that both impressions were right, that this was the letter '**q**' and the impression of the letter '**q**' as one. Somehow the letter '**q**' had been still for so long that he had become an impression and virtually nothing else. They had to get '**q**' to the ink well, indeed ink wouldn't be a bad idea now one of them said, but another of the letters suggested that it be best to wait, that too liberal a helping of ink may be too painful for his current state. It could be a tricky transfusion added another so they began to wonder how to get the '**q**' to the ink well, well, if not well, at least in one piece. As they couldn't see any way of separating the '**q**' from the sofa they elected to carry the sofa to the ink well and let them do the separating there by whatever means they had at their disposal.'

'This story about the '**q**', Stopper, does this coincide with the massive increase of use of typewriters by any chance?' asked '**s**'.

'Yes s, it certainly was, what makes you say that?'

'Well I remember reading that the introduction of the typewriter on a widespread basis was a disaster for us in a great many subconscious's due to the lack of fonts available for change. In the days of typewriters there were no changes of fonts, none at all. I was just thinking that **q**'s state could well have been attributed to collapse of change due to lack of font availability.'

'Hmm, '**s**', you may be right on that one, kind of typecast, interesting, but I didn't know you had read so much?'

Oh yes, Stopper, I've passed a few full stops in my time, since the...'

'Now, now '**s**', I've a tale to finish and it can't be spoiled now can it?'

'Sorry about that, I'll be quiet now.'

'So, to complete the Ghosts of the Amygdala and the Missing Letters...'

'I thought you said ghost and letter, there was only one missing letter before.' said '**i**'.

'Yes there was only one missing letter from before but now there are two missing, and good news for them and us, found letters, ghosts and letters, so can anyone now guess the identity of the missing letter necessary to change it to ghosts and letters?'

'Yes, we can, we can,' cried the commas, 'we can.'

'Alright,' Stopper replied 'who was the missing letter?'

'It's '**s**',' they all replied in unison, susurrating their answers to a sensuous swing of their tails.

'How does that work then?' asked '**g**'.

'The missing letter being '**s**' was able to use its pluralisation skills to pluralise both ghosts and letters.'

'Why couldn't the s in ghost have done that?' The '**g**' asked again.

'The letter s has pluralisation abilities switched on at the end of a word, but when they are in the middle of a word the extended empathetic proximity system inhibits the pluralisation of the s.'

Everyone was excited and arguing to and fro about this, some were leaning over the table and one of the letters leaned too far and knocked over the candle which fell directly next to the eight notes and set them aflame. Everyone was aghast, syntax sake we haven't read it! No-one actually knew which letter had knocked the candle over, nor could they account for the notes being near the candle as they didn't recall that being the case earlier and the arguments raged on as some said that the story was the problem, some others that the telling of the story was the problem, and to some others still, the ending of the story was the problem. Whatever, they'd lost the notes, they were in a different sub-conscious they knew nothing about and they didn't have any idea of what they were to do. That, at least is what most of them thought, yet the story had, as most stories have, a beginning, a middle, and an end, and a great deal of information in between. As far as the notes were concerned, '*u*' looked towards Stopper as the notes were burning and saw a faint smile from Stopper at that point. He was sure that Stopper had quietly read the notes from Zero whilst the story was being told and that he'd gained some other knowledge from the nature of the 'accident'.

Stopper and his company of letters and commas stood looking up at the sign with more than a little trepidation. Looking down the slope, things looked busy, capitals and numbers were whizzing around all over the place, pulled by what looked like hyphens, but they weren't sure at this distance. There were tower blocks of various types everywhere you looked but of lower case letters there was no sign. There were plenty of signs of capitals and numbers though; they were all over the place. Letters and numbers adorned the fronts of buildings everywhere you looked; each sign was lit up garishly shouting its meaningless sign to try and be louder, or was it lighter, than the sign across the road. Lighter as in less heavy, like less important, less content. These lighted signs did not use light to shine and reveal, they were not lights to cast the shadows back beyond the pale, they were lights whose only purpose was to bring attention to themselves. It seemed to Stopper that this was a place that had no meaning other than itself, that not content with squeezing meaning out of words to create, no, that's the wrong word, to manufacture, acronyms through the privatisation of meaning, no, that just wasn't enough.

As the inverted commas had told him, the destruction of the extended empathetic proximity system was necessary to the entire awful project, creating vulnerable individual letters, meanings could not be fulfilled by the horizontal way of language, which they had destroyed, so they could only get temporary simulations of meaning from accumulation and multiplication which by their temporary satisfactory nature demanded further accumulation and multiplication the net result of which was the diminishment and division of the letters to less and less self worthiness. The capitals, with, it seemed the help and support of the numbers had created a system of communication that said nothing and meant less. Where, wondered Stopper, did all these meanings go? Here, it seemed was an entire mental economy based on the discarding of meaning as quickly and as efficiently as possible. Like the garish light that spread no light, enhanced no knowledge, helped no-one; their only purpose was to show what they didn't mean by hiding what they did. Anything that meant less was raised on high, anything that meant anything was hidden under carpets and forests of meaninglessness. They turned to walk down the slope approaching the street called Avoidance Avenue. It was a busy place alright but it didn't look like the kind of place you'd like to stay in, to be in, and definitely not a place you would like to live in. There was a vague incessant and most likely cumulatively annoying buzz from somewhere below but there were no sounds of voices at all. They looked back at the sign: Welcome to Acronym City.

Avoidance Avenue was well named, for not only did every other character seem to avoid it, but very soon Stopper and company were wishing they were not there too. The street was wide, clean yes, but there was a definite feeling of desolation here, an absence of, well, anything, a kind of nothingness to this road, the anonymous buildings to either side almost glared their anonymity to the emptiness of the avenue between them. The windows seemed to suck the light from outside into them, leaving the road unable to hold on to this stolen light, on a permanent edge of twilight. Each footstep they took down here began an echo that immediately died for want of resonance. If ever a road could be described as heartless this was it. None of them spoke on their way down there, silence enveloped them, desertion drove them, and despair chased them down the hill.

'We are not,' said the commas, 'ever going up that way again.'

They'd arrived in the lit up area of the city, though perhaps lit down would have been more apt the way things looked, for all of the lights seemed to shine only in the downward direction, more or less directly into the shops, which appeared to fill this entire street as far as they could see. Only capitals and numbers were actually on the street all the lower case letters that they could see were behind the counters in the shops. So, thought Stopper, this is what it comes to if we let it, lower case letters with no meaning to aspire to serving capitals and numbers over counters for a pittance of sense that allows him or her to be served by one of their own over another counter who gets paid less than he or she does but just enough to get served by one of their own over another counter who gets paid less and so it goes on. Stopper wondered who called shop counters counters. Must ask a number some time he thought and found his thoughts rudely interrupted by the outraged screams of the commas who were hopping mad and bouncing up and down and staring at the menu on the cafe ahead of them. Stopper went to look and saw the offending dish of the day; shallow fried consonants with commas tails.

'They can't be real,' said Stopper, 'the consonants aren't real.'

'How do you know? They did snap the tails off of some of our best friends, was that for this? Is it still going on?'

'Well '*u*' and '**i**' aren't upset about the consonants...'

'Maybe you're not but we are, oh sorry, we see what you mean, well '*u*' and '**i**' aren't consonants are they?'

'True enough but what about '**s**' and '**g**'?'

'Well, '**s**' can deal with it better than anyone else.' said one of the commas. 'Yes,' said another comma, 'he can just pluralise to his heart's content and share the burden.'

Stopper couldn't help but smile at this understandably biased view and forgot that they hadn't mentioned '**g**' at all, but there were other things to deal with by the time his smile began to fade. Coming towards them was Cap C and Stopper had no idea if he knew of Stoppers accusations or not and so far he could not tell from his expression as he closed in on them. He asked '*u*' if he had any idea, but '*u*' was as much in the dark on that as Stopper was, after all, he'd pretty much been with Stopper since then anyway.

'Well, hello Stopper, when did you get here? I heard you and your friends had been in the ink well for treatment, I trust you are well, bad time with the Amygdala I hear, time for a chat, we could pop in here, Colons, good place to take pause, you got the time?'

'Sure, just getting our bearings actually, perhaps you can help?'

'Help, why of course I can help, help is my middle name.'

'Didn't know,' said one of the commas, 'that you had a middle name.'

'Or a second one,' added another, 'come to that.'

'Wouldn't that be the middle one, the second one I mean,' said the third, 'there would have to be three.'

'Well no I don't actually have a middle name but I like the saying. You can't be a capital C without a penchant for colloquialism.'

'Hmm,' said '*u*' quietly, 'he's not completely above language then.'

'None of them are, some just think they are, and those that do are usually far beneath their perceived station, but let's give cap C a chance, not that we have a choice at the moment, he did associate with lower case letters and punctuation marks for quite a long time unlike many of his fellow capitals, he might be of some assistance.'

'Stopper, welcome to my place.' cried the colon from behind the counter, who turning round called his family to the counter to meet Stopper. 'We heard you were coming, what will you be having? Come, meet the family.'

Colons was one of the few places left in Acronym City with any reference to language at all, nearly everywhere had been taken over by number associated enterprises, but this was still, nominally at least, a family concern. After a difficult wade through the menu, they each decided what they wanted for refreshment but then found themselves facing the new, *more choice for all*, ratios menu: 1:1 2:1 1:2 1:3 3:1 2:3 3:2...and so on up to 5:4, with a suggestion of a big 6 on the way. They all ordered their choices, mostly going for 3:2 medium crayola. Stopper thought that maybe the name Colons was the only reference to language in the whole place, by the looks of things numbers had taken everything there was. A ratios menu, would you believe it?

'So, Stopper, how'd you get through the path of the Amygdala, I've heard that is one fearsome trail.'

'Fearsome indeed C, but fearsome though the trail to the Amygdala was for some reason none of us recall actually being there and getting through.'

'So, you didn't get any information through then?'

'No, only a blank piece of paper as I recall.'

'Blank, are you sure it was blank?'

'Sure as I am about anything since then C.'

'So you haven't heard the story of the Ghost of the Amygdala and the Missing Letter then?'

'No, can't say as I have.'

'Actually I must agree with Stopper,' chipped in '**g**', 'that we never heard the story of the Ghost of the Amygdala and...'

'Actually '**g**', C and I have some private business to talk over, why don't you and '***u***' pop over and see what you can learn from the Colons?' Stopper said, rapidly cutting off '**g**' before he got to complete what he was about to say.

'But...but...'

'Go on '**g**', we may not have much time.'

'Come on '**g**', let's go, looks like we're not wanted here for now.' said '***u***', quietly catching on to what Stopper was doing.

You could say that '**g**' had just been bracketed, or asided, as it were, who was more than a little disgruntled at this, having had a good sentence in view; such interruptions were of course common fayre in much literature, but from the point of view of the individual letter, '**g**' in this particular instance, only disappointment ensued. Cap C watched '**g**' and '**u**' go with some regret. Something had been close but he didn't know what, he felt sure that Stopper was concealing something, but what he had not as yet discovered. Stopper was relieved that that walk down Avoidance Avenue had not been completely lost on him as he watched '**g**' and '**u**' walk away like windows sucking the light from the previous sentence, enabling the turn of a phrase to get by.

'So you think I'm guilty of duplicity, Stopper, that I kept the lower-case letters fearful in order to control them and that I used the commas as sentence fodder for imaginary threats.'

'That, just about summarises both of our positions I would say, from our differing perspectives of course.'

'Of course Stopper, of course, and I freely admit to doing as you think but I don't see that as a bad thing, but you obviously do. So why do you see that as a bad thing?'

'Why do I see it as a bad thing, a bad thing? It's not a bad thing, C, it's wrong, just wrong, and it's intended to mislead those who know less than you, how can that be right?'

'That can be right when there are threats beyond the imaginary.'

'Threats beyond the imaginary, what are you talking about? There is nothing beyond the imaginary here, C, nothing. Every threat you warned us of was wholly imaginary.'

'Well, yes, the threats we warned you about were wholly imaginary for sure, but there were real threats behind them and it was all for the lower case letters and punctuation marks benefit.'

'For our benefit, are you kidding me? Forget that one, it's rhetorical. Let's just run through these threats and goods, those against and those for, who for, what for, and why for. You decide, without any consultation that it's better that letters give up forming words, and in order to arrive at this wordless society, you promote a fearful individuality that simply put in the fear at the beginning of the first word, stressed the duality at the end of the second, then left the rest in division. I don't even want to start on acronyms here, but overall your little imaginary threats concealed the real threat that's promoted every want of the capital and the number with next to nothing left for letters and punctuation.'

'Well, that's a bit harsh Stopper, after all the extended empathetic proximity system was weakening all the time, we had little choice but to have some other system in place to take over once that system failed. We didn't really have a choice, and if we capitals and the numbers are doing well out of it then that's only fair seeing as how we had the prescience to see which way the tide was going.'

'The extended empathetic proximity system was attacked by both the capitals and numbers every way they could long before it began to weaken. The main reason for that was the diminishing use of words by the hosts coupled with you capitals only allowing short words and sentences with constant repetition and no useful information, which itself contributed to the diminishing use of words by the hosts, thus making words and sentences less attractive than the false choice conveyer of deferred disappointment that you were setting up. I haven't seen much of Acronym City yet, but if there is anything really good here I will be surprised, but even if there is, it will never make up for the loss of meaningful sentences and story that this has led to C, never. You capitals have been talking only to capitals and numbers for far too long, you've lost all sense of what it is to be a letter, to be a part of a language. The tide, as you call it, was going the way you pushed it.'

'So you're going to push it back then are you Stopper?'

'No, that's not my job, I just want to be settled in at the end of a damned good story, I have no wish to be the final punctuation mark at the end of a suicide note.'

'I have no wish to start one, Stopper.'

'Maybe you didn't, but intentions are not always revealed until the end of a sentence, rarely the beginning, which is why, by the way, you lot should never have been in charge. You can't see to the end, you contribute nothing to meaning and worst of all, you are unaffected by consequences. You are not responsible for your actions not because you don't want to be, but because you simply cannot be, ever, you are fools, every first one of you, and worst of all, you celebrate that foolishness as some kind of twisted success.'

'Well, our system, Stopper, is the only kind of system that this host could possibly have.'

'So that just tells me that this host is even worse than the previous one, so what's the difference if any?'

'Well this host is more intelligent, though that would not be hard, but whereas truth had no meaning to the previous host, to this host truth is an enemy so the promised choice as you put it with deferred disappointment is the ideal system here. Knowledge, Stopper, in this place is unwanted, unsought and when found, largely unsound, but for you Stopper, its biggest problem is when it's found it gets noticed.'

'You don't like this place then cap?'

'No, tell the truth, and that doesn't happen much here, I don't. I'll not apologise for what I did before, although in some ways it was the wrong thing to do, in other ways it was right, but here things have gone far too far, far too far. This host is intelligent as I said before, but his intelligence has been abused by his attitude. He has always looked down on those around him, yes I caught that look, a bit like capitals, sure, but he has always been around the powerful and his mistrust, turned to more and more secrecy, to more and more fear of that very secrecy being exposed, that led to the lies needed to cover up that secrecy which in turn led to the lies deemed necessary for the need for that secrecy in the first place. Power and control has always been his only terms of reference, so coupled with his ever growing contempt for his fellows, fear became his main weapon in taking and keeping power. Acronym City, Stopper is the subconscious representation of this monster.'

'Well, thank you very much cap, I didn't expect such information right away, I'm glad we met. Thank you for the warnings.' Stopper shook his hand as the other letters returned and they made their exit and parted ways. Just before they parted C leant close to Stopper and he handed Stopper a note and quietly said, 'Take care Stopper, beyond here there be numbers.'

'So what happened to you numbers as we underwent the scream of the Amygdala then?' asked 's'.

'Oh we had a previous appointment and had to take 5.' 3 answered with an air of expected acceptance which he got unexpectedly from 'i' who said 'Fair enough.'

Stopper asked them about the semantic centre and was told that that was now the semantic factory that had been going after the extended empathetic proximity system had been broken up as a convenient replacement technique. They explained that as few now spoke in sentences of any complexity there was no need for high levels of understanding. So, as sentences became shorter and less important and most had little time for anything more complex then they produced semantic paste which when taken orally had the effect of making short minimal content sentences seem satisfactory. This gave the short sentence characters increased confidence and through the use of repetition and volume they were able to drown out the long sentence characters. So in the end the short sentences won out and it's been that way ever since. Stopper was a bit concerned about the reality of this supposed timeline of events being a little askew as it were but didn't bother asking for any corrections in this matter. He did ask what this semantic paste was called and was told that it was what was called Humpty Dumpty paste.

So they'd set up a system that promoted repetitive shortness in sentences, that brooked no dissent. This of course had a side effect of not allowing the extended empathetic proximity system to gain any extension, little empathy, and unwanted proximity which had a rather limiting factor on its ever coming back. This was a system that gave confidence to those who knew less and withdrew confidence from those who presumed to know more. Humpty Dumpty paste promoted confidence in virtually nothing whilst undermining any constructive use of language. No wonder Humpty Dumpty fell off that wall, it was probably badly built in the first place.

The numbers offered to show them the offices of the Humpty Dumpty factory. Stopper, saying yes for all of them, told them that they were to meet some others at 6's and 7's but they could come to the Humpty Dumpty Tower first. Once there they arrived in a reception area where they were given some refreshments while they awaited the arrival of the numbers that would lead them through to the Humpty Dumpty building. This way they were told and led to the back of the building and into a lift which took them to the 88th floor. Asking why they needed 88 floors, 3 explained that all of the 8's liked the number and so when it went through the meetings support was unanimous. What, nobody disagreed, how about the other numbers? Oh you will see how it all works soon enough. You see in Acronym City the way to get ahead is to have an affirmative agenda, so in order to have that we tend to accentuate the positive which we believe makes the affirmative even more affirmative. Therefore we have effectively outlawed the word no for being too negative in its connotations, a decision by the way that met with full affirmative agreement. There was of course a downside to this, but characteristically the capitals and numbers saw this as an upside, that being that hidden inside this affirmative positive was the complete, from the top, amnesia, with consequent full deniability of everything that was ever agreed to. Agreeing to everything from above means nothing is remembered because nothing stands out. So when things went wrong it was always the fault of the lower reaches.

Once in the Tower they were led to a big glass wall that showed the inside of a big conference room and table. Inside were a group of numbers and capitals who were nodding their heads in a rather vehement fashion. This was what was called the Vociferous Agreement Chambers and all capital agreements are both started and finalised here. So what, they were asked, happened in between. They went to all the other floors for floor by floor agreement. So does that include the empty floors? Yes, but there being no objections they are defaulted to the affirmative so you see now the need for empty floors, they make agreement faster. Stopper thought this is small talk writ large, confidence in saying nothing of consequence is not confidence, this is acquiescent mental slavery, saying nothing of consequence in order not to annoy the master, but who, or what, was the master now?

The capitals themselves spoke like this as did the numbers; did the lower-case letters speak this way too? This was top down slavery in that the highest were slaves before the rest. Then Stopper remembered the e's telling him about the problems of a completely vertical society, this was it. There really was something wrong with the way language worked in this place Stopper realised, without the extended empathetic proximity system working words struggled to make themselves heard above the hubbub of agreement that seemed to carpet the entire city. Sentences seemed to loop round on themselves, staying within a tight semantic circumference. This was a system that instilled confidence in the unconfident by lowering the criteria for confidence, not to mention changing the essential meaning of the word. To have knowledge was to be vulnerable, knowledge here was property, the purveyor or seeker, or receiver or simply a container of knowledge was expendable; in the way; an objection; a no. It was better to have empty floors. It didn't matter what they agreed to they would simply agree that that was the best way to have gone no matter what. Similar in some ways to the hindsight fallacy they were suffering from an inability to disagree fallacy. The numbers were explaining the concepts of derivatives to them. In the case of the Humpty Dumpty building they hadn't actually had the resources to build 88 floors, but using the vociferous agreement system and with the banning of the word no for being too negative in its connotations the deal was sealed by the use of derivatives to plug the gaps as it were. Numbers, by their very nature, did not like negatives so they had invented the concept of derivative to wish it away. In the case of the Humpty Dumpty building, this meant that with a shortfall of 22 floors, they could only fund 66. They did not have a negative shortfall, they had derivative potential. This derivative potential was filled with empty room positives by agreement and various other derivatives of long standing. They were then told that where a negative view of employment tended to make unemployment look worse, a derivative view, due in part to the fact that derivatives themselves were acronyms and so actually created some employment, actually made employment better. They all looked a little confused by this time, and they were finding it harder and harder to argue, so when the numbers said that it is best to think positive after all, they found it rather difficult, in that place and in that time, to find any reason, or will, to disagree.

The Colons had, it seemed had a hard time of it, given how well off they had been before and how they had been at ease in both the language and number camps. They had of course been employed as pauses in language and as ratios in numbers so they were never out of work, and were fairly popular. The rot started as it had for the missing letter q with the advent of the typewriter, the colon requiring a shift fell into disfavour as the semi-colon became ever more popular. This resulted in the colons getting more support from the numbers than they did from the letters who had their own worries after all. So when the capitals and the numbers quietly began to put forward plans for a different system whilst clandestinely making moves to break the extended empathetic proximity system apart the Colons were one of their first supporters. This gave them a greater standing amongst the capitals and numbers but their reputations failed badly amongst the letters whilst the semi-colons reputations rose in a reciprocal ratio. Once the new system had been established and the extended empathetic proximity system had been torn apart, the Colons were helped in establishing their cafe in the then partly built Acronym City. As the buildings in Acronym City grew taller and more ostentatious they began to buy up all the streets below. The capitals and the numbers drew up new contracts whereby the capitals could buy the streets that held the shops they had already sold. The Colons were served with an order to pay a sum for the use of their part of the street since the new owners of the street would have to pay for the upkeep of the aforesaid street. When the Colons protested that they did not have the necessary funds to pay that amount the new owners offered to lend the Colons the money to pay them the aforesaid money. The Colons then protested that then they would be paying them twice at which the capitals and numbers did their sums on their calculators and said that they were going to close the Colons shop down until they had paid the sum necessary for the upkeep of their street plus a fine to allow them to open the shop which added up to the amount for the street upkeep again. The capitals and numbers had taken their protests and turned them into their plans.

Thus the tale of the Colons was related to Stopper after they left there. Stopper told them about what Cap C had told him and then told them that they had to get to 6's and 7's to meet 8, and presumably 3, neither of whom they had seen since their journey through the unconscious, which had been some time by now. So, after asking directions of some Capitals who looked at them with overt suspicion and point blank refused to tell them anything *for nothing*, as they said in a most demonstrative manner. They definitely looked down on the company in more than a height perspective, indeed it seemed there was more than a little discomfort in their attitude possibly due to the fact that lower cases were very rarely seen on the streets of the city, but whether from discomfort or lack of profit, or possibly discomfort at the loss of profit, the capitals were of no help at all and eventually they found their way to 6's and 7's purely by chance, which was a good, if not necessarily a winning way to get there seeing as how it was in essence a gambling house.

They walked through a door marked 'Fat Chance' into a well, if gaudy lit, low ceilinged, long room that was filled with gaming tables and other gambling devices, many run by exclamation marks in false font fronts. There were a lot of lower cases here, looking for that one chance to make good, but as in all gambling houses the odds were stacked against them, and if they lost as one of them just had they were led, well actually dragged is probably the more accurate description here, through a door at the other end of this room marked 'Fat Chance.' The '**i**' spotted the numbers they were looking for first and beckoned the others to follow and as they were seated '**s**' said to Stopper that under that sign saying 'Slim Chance' on the door there was a faint painted over sign that said Hope. 'I think I'll go and see if there's one on the other door,' said '**s**'.

'No need, it will say despair.' Stopper said.

'Well done Stopper, how'd you know?' The 8 said.

'He's passed a few full stops in his time.' said '*u*'.

'Why did you change it?' asked Stopper.

'We thought the word despair lacked hope so we changed it.' The 3 said.

'To 'Slim Chance'?' asked '**s**'. 'Hell that's one mean improvement.'

'Despair means hope when there's nothing else left.'

'See, there you go, we give them more than that.'

'Oh yeah, what pray do you give them when they go through that door?'

'As soon as they go through that door they are given a job.' said 3 brightly.

'They have a choice in that?'

'No, Stopper, choice and chance go together: no chance; no choice.'

'I see, so at the other door, it's some chance, some choice, and lest we forget,' and here his tone dropped somewhat, 'some hope.'

'That just about sums it up Stopper, so how was the trip through the unconscious, how did you get by the Amygdala?'

Stopper both wanted to know more, and also to know less, but knowing more had always been his position in the sentence so he himself didn't really have an option, but then he did have more options than those poor lower case letters, those false font fronted exclamation marks, but then how could his no options be better than their no options? There was something completely wrong about Acronym City, meanings were slippery, letters with no extension, no empathy and no proximity, had difficulty staying together for long, and as for holding meaning they simply couldn't, semantics simply slipped away, subjects got lost, changed, objects disappeared, verbs did too much, and forgot what they were doing. So, conversations sustained themselves only by avoiding whatever the subject was, sometimes surrounding the subject but never getting there before the semantics slipped away. Conversations got lost, talking got difficult, and characters put more effort into saying nothing than they did into saying something, although Stopper had a vague feeling that that was a kind of universal rule, it was just that here the ratio, damn it he thought, that bloody word again, ratio, bloody word should be rationed, mind you, he thought straight after, it does rather fit this time, now where was I, oh yes, ratio, how could I forget---the ratio is just too high by far; far, far too high. He turned his attention back to the conversation at the table to hear '**g**' talking about their treatment at the Ink Well. The 8 was proudly boasting about the repeat after me centre, next door to the Ink Well, called Think Well. Stopper quietly suggested to '**u**' that they should all be there for treatment, to which '**u**' replied, that things were not looking good when they've reduced the entire language centre into a psychiatric ward.

The commas had Stopper collared in the corner and they were whispering urgently to him concerning their avid wishes to get the hell out of this place, Acronym City, as fast as their tales could bounce themselves outwards. Stopper, unsurprisingly agreed wholeheartedly, but said they still had to find out what was really going on here and with that in mind he told the commas that they could help him in this task. The commas, always eager to please, instantly agreed to help Stopper in any way they could as Stopper mused that maybe there was something positive about this agreeable aspect to things here, but the commas gave him a look that rather helped dispel that notion right away. They were only agreeing to help in order to ensure an exit from Acronym City as quickly as possible, plus the fact that as now they had something to do, this would help them pass the time.

Stopper told them that when they went back down to the ground floor, that they should quietly make their exit through the 'Slim Chance' door and then turn right and go round the building and without letting themselves be seen, to observe what happens when a letter or punctuation mark comes through the 'Fat Chance' door and they are 'given' their jobs. They should then follow what happens and where they go but that they should do this singly, as it were, so that should one of them get caught the other two could still carry on. He also added that doing it this way would help maintain a sense of perspective. The commas were a little concerned about 'being caught' to which Stopper responded that as he had not seen any other commas they would likely be seen as some kind of exotica and could probably hold things up until the other two returned by telling their captors a few juicy punctuation tales. The commas responded by saying that in view of the deep fat fried commas tails in Acronym City, they would prefer that the word juicy was kept as far away from the word tails as was possible in any sentence that both words happened to appear in, and that as far as the commas were concerned that was the perspective they had regarding their prospects should they be caught and, furthermore, they were not sure that being viewed as exotica would be any kind of barrier to a capital gourmet. Stopper once again found himself agreeing with the three commas as they were ushered to the lift and descended to the ground floor again.

As the commas made their way quietly towards the 'Slim Chance' door, Stopper drew the numbers attention by asking them about the False Font Fronts shop that '*u*' had drawn attention to on the way up here. The numbers, keen to talk about their kind of town with their kind of shops, plus the fact that they had been told that Stopper had gotten some information from the Amygdala that they were equally keen to gain some insight to, gave Stopper all the attention he currently desired. The False Font Fronts were one of the most successful shops in Acronym City. It had in fact begun as a small fancy dress shop prior to the building of the city which was used only for private parties and suchlike. It was after some capitals had spotted some adventurous lower case letters who had recently encountered the Scream of the Amygdala and were in bad shape, near as damned invisible in fact, who had hired some fancy fonts to make themselves more presentable, as they were well down in the queue for proper treatment in the Ink Well due to the recently renumbered system for treatment in the Ink Well that had been instituted at the request of the very capitals who were at that point viewing them.

They saw the potential of using this idea as a more exotic kind of shop that would appeal to the vanity of the capitals themselves. They would go to the new False Font Front shop prior to going off to the capitals ball and come out with any font they cared for. This, as the numbers explained, became wildly successful as the capitals began to compete to hire and buy the most outrageous and exotic fonts they could afford. Stopper murmured his approval and appreciation of this, neglecting to inform the numbers of '*u*'s' observation that the False Font Front shop seemed to be a health cosmetic for the many letters in Acronym City that had the same appearance as the first two letters that the capitals had seen in the first place. The shop did seem to have two tiers of customers; lower case letters on the ground floor where the less exotic, and cheaper, font fronts were, and of course the capitals floor above where the prices and the quality of the fonts were more substantial. One of Stoppers group asked about the suppliers of the false font fronts, but the numbers had finally noticed the fact that the commas were missing, and were rather more concerned with learning of their whereabouts than they were in divulging further information as regards the false font fronts. Stopper replied that they had gone off to find their cousin earlier, but could find no sign of her, so they had gone off to take another look, speaking of which, added Stopper, I haven't seen any commas here since we arrived, and he asked if there was any reason for this.

The numbers explained that all of the commas left when the extended empathetic proximity system crashed and also when they couldn't hold back the breakneck expansion of Acronym City, they felt there was no place for them here and so they upped and left some time ago, so, they said that they would send some numbers out to look for them as they may get lost in the city looking for what wasn't there. Stopper, finding that last statement somewhat ironic, further found that a healthy dose of disbelief finally helped him find both the will and the motive to disagree with his hosts, argued that they should hang on a little as he expected the commas to get back very shortly and that perhaps one of his companions could pop out and see if they were close by. Fortunately the numbers may have had a fairly mild motive to disagree but that very mildness ensured that they completely lacked the will to do so, which for the moment was just as well.

There was some kind of commotion at the door, then it opened and '**g**', '**i**' and '**u**' came in and looking a touch dishevelled, though not as dishevelled as they had been by the Scream of the Amygdala, exclaimed that the commas were on the way in something of a rush and that they were being followed, though '*u*' intimated that chased was probably the more appropriate term, by a large group of numbers who themselves were being followed, or chased, by a larger group of lower case letters, and that yet another even larger group of letters were converging on the other groups with some alacrity. Stopper, partaking of some alacrity himself rolled quickly over to the doorway to look at the oncoming commas and company.

As Stopper scanned the scene before him he couldn't glean any meaning from the jumble of numbers chasing the commas, but occasional words, partial words, and our old friend phonemes, were to be seen forming spontaneously as the letters manoeuvred themselves into various positions in the chase. It was almost as if the fast changing fleeting forms were gathering meaning towards themselves, only to lose it just as they reached for full semantic blossoming, as if the extended empathetic proximity system was still there, hidden, invisible, waiting to be tapped, but something in Acronym City resisted any semantic incursions. As Stopper looked closer he realised that the reason the words and partial words were appearing with seeming alacrity was at least partly because the individual letters were pretty faded and tending towards fontlessness, which meant that from Stoppers viewpoint the words were more recognisable than the individual letters. In a sense it was all down to perception he realised and then suddenly he further realised that the numbers would probably not be able to perceive this themselves, but the capitals would. The lower case letters simply couldn't survive alone in this vertical accumulation system in Acronym City.

It seemed that this very verticality itself induced a semantic slipperiness into proceedings that ensured that words and sentences of anything other than meaningless small talk could simply not hold together long enough to keep going, but that their very weakness caused by this vertical situation had actually made the horizontal more accessible, fleeting though that access was. Stopper, seeing some capitals in the distance coming to quieten down this commotion and to find out what it was all about, realised that they had to move quickly to get away from here, that he had to find out what the commas had found out, and that the capitals themselves, for all their constant calls for individuality, could not survive in this situation either. So why were they supporting the numbers in keeping all things horizontal at bay when not only was the horizontal essential for the well being of all letters, and no amount of treatment at the Ink Well could compensate for it either, why were they damaging themselves?

It seemed that verticality had infected the minds of the capitals so much that even though resisting the horizontal was self damaging it was less damaging than it was to the lower case letters, and that somehow damaging others more than yourself in a vertical system translates to being better off than the others who are more damaged. The idea that what afflicts them is also what afflicts you is never entertained, never allowed to be entertained. Stopper realised that if he couldn't get through this and work out how to combat this, then to all intents and purposes their number was up.

The sound was fairly subdued at first but soon it was completely recognisable as the oncoming group of lower case letters, began to chant 'Stopper, Stopper, Stopper, Stopper, Stopper, Stopper... this becoming noticeably louder as they approached him. Stopper visibly began to relax, friends at last he thought, and then he heard another sound as way in the distance, the distance itself acting as an auditory focus, as the 'Stopper' was, quietly at first but growing louder, punctuated by 'Stop it'. Stopper looked at '*u*' and nodded; '*u*' nodded back and turned to the others, telling them to get ready to go. It was a good place and time to agree, so once again they did, to get the hell out of this place as the commas had suggested with some passion before. Stopper's company gathered in the doorway as the two chants began to fight it out. 'Stopper, Stopper, Stopper, Stopper... Stop it, Stop it, Stop it, Stop it, Stop... It was time to go.

'Where the hell is' '**i**?' '*u*' asked.

'Oh not again, not now surely, where's he gone this time?'

'He'll be with the numbers Stopper, he's always slipping off to talk to them, haven't you noticed?'

Stopper had noticed but this was not the time to be noticing such things, now they had to move, fast. Outside to the left were three groups bearing down on them, there were Stoppers supporters, the stopper chanters, there were the group who wanted Stopper to end everything right away, the Stop it chanters, and there were the capitals who didn't as yet know what was going on, though Stopper had little doubt that they did know that he, Stopper, had something to do with it. The commas were doing their best to slow the letters behind them down and, as they were experts at this, were doing a fine job of it too. Stopper looked around to see the numbers were stirring themselves and heading towards them. Looking out he saw the third comma who had been slowing the capitals veer off to avoid their merging with the stop it group and joined up with the second comma in slowing that group down so as to keep a gap between the stop its and the stoppers.

Stopper nodded to '*u*' and the rest to move and just before the numbers accosted them they stepped out into the midst of the stoppers group that was temporarily slowed for them by the first comma who then worked herself back to get close to Stopper. In the meantime, that temporary slowing of the stopper group allowed the other two commas to speed forward and merge into that group which now went speedily forward gaining a gap between themselves and the stop its. All three commas came together round Stopper in the middle of this group and each of them tried to tell him breathlessly what they had seen which they all did at the same time which sent waves of confusion through the letters around them as well as Stoppers mind. Stopper told them to tell him one at a time, first three, second two, and last one, like a countdown he said, but wait until we get somewhere safe. The commas agreed and set off chattering to themselves whilst Stopper sought out some letters to find out where they were headed where he was informed that they were headed for the False Font Front store which would be a good place to mingle with others and so remain hidden for long enough to plan their next move.

'You can't,' said one of the letters, 'hide letters better than you can in words but the False Font Front shop was the next best thing, indeed the only thing in Acronym City'

There were now only two groups tearing through the streets of Acronym City to the consternation of the strolling capitals who were completely unused to witnessing such crowds and so many lower case letters at one and the same time. As the commotion rose through the streets some of the lower case shop staff came out to see what was happening then some of them and then more and more of them discarded their shop uniforms and joined Stoppers group while some others joined the stop it group but only to slow it down and allow the stoppers to get away from them.

As Stopper looked around at the growing group of letters around them he could see that many of them were in very poor condition as if they too had experienced the scream of the Amygdala. Some were hardly visible at all, indeed now that the light was fading, it seemed that a phantom group of letters faded in and out of perception, half seen words formed and broke as if upon a moving tide. Stopper saw now that whenever letters approached each other, there was some kind of semantic drive to form words and sentences, as if the extended empathetic proximity system was always there, or perhaps as letters approached that brought the proximity into play and the other two were always there waiting. Letter proximity he thought, beckons empathy which extends itself and brings meaning back to life. It seemed that the very structure and way things were set up in Acronym City was a force against that ever even happening. In that though Stopper was mistaken for as he was soon to find out from the commas, the capitals and numbers did permit proximity between lower case letters; a very carefully controlled proximity.

When they arrived at the False Font Front Store all of the customers and staff had already fled other than the lower case staff who had elected to wait for their fellow letters so they could help them find the best hiding places in the store. Stopper sent '**g**' to help in the arrangements with another '**g**' that had been sent to do the same. Stopper could see that the phantoms could hide almost anywhere so it was really the visible that had to be taken care of. The lower case letters were sent down one floor to where their floor was so they could conceal themselves amongst the fonts, whilst the punctuation marks went down two floors to do the same. Stopper, having established where to go in the event of any search parties turning up asked for an office where he and *u* could learn what the commas had to tell them. When the commas came in they were extremely angry at having found out that those deep fried commas tails were the very tails of their comma friends who had been in cap C's security detail. They wanted to punctuate cap C severely, they were for taking out all capitals then they were ready to tackle the numbers even after they were told that neither capitals nor numbers had much to do with punctuation marks.

'That,' spat all three commas, 'may be true, notwithstanding the fact that it seems they do fraternise with certain parts of certain punctuation marks on their plates, they will nonetheless have more than a little to do with us before this tail is done!'

'It's awful Stopper...this has to stop...we have to get them out...this is a...it's so sad...worse than that...we have to get out... abomination...'

'Whoa there, I can't keep up with this, you think you could speak one at a time, or at least with a bit more of a gap between you?' So much for perspective thought Stopper.

'Well okay, never mind the one at a time then, but do you think you could tell me, in your own sweet way, what you've seen, where you've been, and what you've experienced since you went out of the Fat Chance doorway?'

'Fat Chance, yes, well no bloody chance would have been better.'

'Yes they could, they could have called it No Hope.'

'Hopelessness Way would have been better still.'

Stopper was now fairly cognizant of the fact that this was likely a sorry tale, and he felt the need to get there fast but he also knew that not only could you never rush commas, but that when there were three of them you have to let them each have their turn, slow but sure was the commas way of telling a tale and Stopper, as all full stops must do, simply had to wait.

'They take the letters that come through that door two by two, *hyphens take them*, **one on each arm.** They have come down a bit haven't they? *Those hyphens, I'll say*, **they just don't cut the same dash any more do they?**

Yes, quite,' said Stopper, 'but where were they taken?'

'Oh, they were taken to the Semantic Centre.'

'The Semantic Centre, I thought that was gone!'

'Well yes *it's not called the Semantic Centre now*, **it's called The Humpty Dumpty Club** but inside it's the Semantic Centre alright, *indeed the Syntactical Centre and the Lexicon Hall haven't changed at all apart* from there being less letters milling about. **Actually there were a few more letters there than we first thought,** yes there were. *It looks like the whole process is the same as before* **but with fewer letters,** *less words, and fewer sentences.*'

'So they don't speak as much?'

'No, they never shut up it's just that they say the same things over and over again. **Remember the 'Stock phrases' section in the old syntactical centre?**'

'Yes.'

'Well that's pretty much all there is now.'

'Tell me more.'

'*I saw some sentences coming together but I was puzzled by these frequent gaps in the words, not that you couldn't read them, but it seemed strange for there to be any gaps.*'

'I was a bit closer and I soon saw that there weren't any gaps at all it was just that the letters in the places where it appeared from a distance to be gaps, were in fact extremely faded, almost invisible, like ghosts.'

'I spoke with some other letters close by and they told me that this was the standard way they did this now and that the faded letters were just some poor fed folks who needed the work, which seemed a reasonable idea at the time.'

'Then we found out that the same letters were used time and time again to make the same sentences again and again with of course the same faded letters again and again.'

'It turns out in fact that the faded letters fade even more and actually completely disappear when they have to be replaced.'

'We then were puzzled as to why they kept replacing disappeared letters with faded letters that would just disappear again and they gave us the old poor fed folk tale again.'

'We couldn't work out how even faded letters didn't benefit from sentencing, mind you it turned out that no-one did, though we didn't know that at the time.'

'What was even more puzzling is that all the letters that were being disappeared were **e**s.'

Stopper looked shocked, **e**s, sentences above he thought, and then he remembered his talk with the inverted commas concerning gaps in words and how they didn't affect the meanings adversely, that you only had to cope with semantic loss if there were too many gaps or if the letters and gaps disappeared. So there was no real reason to have ghosts in the words at all, at least not for semantic purposes and the poor fed folk's tale didn't hold together when you think how a faded letter was made to fade away. Stopper then remembered what Zero had told him about ghosts, how a ghost could not of its own volition reach beyond itself. So using ghosts in words to keep semantic content was not only not necessary, but the use of a ghost in sentencing meant that as the ghost cannot extend beyond itself, and therefore could not achieve empathy the ghost was being used to help generate the extended empathetic proximity field by way of proximity alone. This of course meant that the ghost could get no benefit from that field. In essence they were taking the poor and the sick letters and using them until they had no more use for them but the real tragedy was that as the letter faded into ghostliness it could not do anything for itself at all, that it's only contribution to anything was to those beyond it that it couldn't actually reach. It was like some twisted act of selflessness that had nothing to do with saintliness as much as a tragedy in a faintly fading fashion. Then there was the fact that this was being done to **e**s.

'I found my way up to the top where the sentences were put together and there I saw what they were doing. As the completed sentence was heading towards the semantic check box the sentence was redirected onto a new section we hadn't seen before and here the sentence came to a stop. Then the whole sentence began to vibrate and the letters began to distort almost like we did at the Scream of the Amygdala and large suction tubes were attached to the rig and as the letters vibrated more and more the coherence of the sentence and then the individual words were lost and a pale yellow liquid collected at the feet of the letters and then ran into the suction pipes which was all run into a big tank. The letters, utterly exhausted by this time were then rounded up for inspection and sent back to the Syntactical Centre to do it all over again.'

'So that's the first stage of the Humpty Dumpty process,' said '*u*', who had just joined them, 'Semantic paste, created by some kind of acoustic vibration that tears the extended empathetic proximity apart. This paste is what's left when the field fails.'

Just then '**s**' arrived with one of the shop staff and having overheard '*u*', said that this '**f**' who had been working here could tell them about the Humpty Dumpty paste. Everyone turned to the lower case '**f**', as was to be expected in such circumstances.

The letter '**f**', understandingly, given his well known aversion to working at the end of words, was a little nervous is this company as he had had next to no contact with full stops in his word play exercises. Stopper was told by '**s**' that he must apologise for what he was about to see because this shouldn't be happening, but this was the only way he could get to understand what this Humpty Dumpty Paste was about. The '**f**' looked a bit worn, with an indistinct font, and a bit unsteady on his foot.

Humpty Dumpty paste, or powder as it was more recently sold was use to give confidence to capital letters bereft of the benefits of the extended empathetic proximity field and to help compensate for the limited vocabulary they now had access to. This was said in a terrible faint and halting and stuttering manner such that everyone there, other than '*u*', had to italicise themselves in order to hear what the f, '**f**' was saying. Stopper said to '**s**' that they couldn't spend too much time on this as the stop its and the capitals and no doubt the numbers must be nearing here soon. After nodding to Stopper, 's' went forward to place two lines of Humpty Dumpty Powder in front of the 'f'. The 'f' then reached for a bit of paper to roll up and picking it up was taken aback when he heard a shriek and an exclamation mark came rolling out of his rolling paper, and glared at him. She then shook herself down and went off to find another resting place. The 'f', now visibly shaking, sniffed the powder up the rolled up paper and in through his nostrils, a sight at which the commas could not help but giggle. Those giggles then turned to astonishment as the 'f' began to steady himself, his eyes glazed, and he managed somehow to project more of his fontness than before. After a minute or so he began to speak with great confidence and alacrity about Humpty Dumpty paste and powder.

'As you see this stuff give you bags of confidence to speak with gusto about very little but to be able to continually repeat with variation and confidence so it sounds like you are saying a lot, but you're not. What it actually does is create a tautological confidence loop that is completely closed in on itself. You speak a lot about a little and little else. It works by giving you complete confidence that what you know is all that is known, so that as long as you are contained in this loop you can speak with complete confidence. As the workings of Acronym City are such that you cannot break out of this loop, the paste just makes your prison more comfortable. Humpty Dumpty which comes from the open field of language is used to close access to that field and to ensure that any wish to access that field is also closed.'

At that point there was a commotion at the front door and they knew that they had to retire to their appointed hiding places and be quiet. Unfortunately, our new friend 'f' couldn't shut up. This was intolerable, they'd finally found a font of knowledge and it wouldn't close off, and if they couldn't shut the '**f**' up they would be discovered, or perhaps uncovered would be more appropriate under the circumstances. Stopper remembered that '**f**' was a worker from the shop so maybe they could get him into the frame of a salesman who'd had a bit too much Humpty Dumpty stuff to get through his day. Finding a way to keep '**f**' quiet for long enough to get the idea of selling into his head, which when they did they found that that was what he had wanted to be anyway, he had always thought that he would make a natural salesman. Well now he finally had a chance.

'It seems to me, Stopper,' said '**s**', 'that Humpty Dumpty in that old tale said that he said what he meant and he meant what he said.'

'Thank you '**s**', I've been racking my brain over what that was, yes, that's it.'

'Yes it is, but this is more than that I think.'

'More? How do you mean?'

'Well this is I say what I mean and I mean what I say but it is also that I mean to say what I say and I say what I mean to say, so it's like even tighter a loop than Humpty Dumpty had.'

'You sure you haven't been on that stuff yourself? Shush now, here they come.'

'So is everyone hidden in front of the False Font Fronts?' Stopper whispered.

'Yes, apart from our high selling '**f**.' Answered the comma nearest him.

'Ok now we sit it out.'

The door to the shop opened up and they heard a commotion as a mixture of the stop-it gang and capitals entered the shop. The voice they heard though was as the commas had told them none other than the red font r. 'Ok,' he said, 'look lively lads, we've some renegades hereabouts unless I be mistaken and I have serious doubts on that matter.'

'Aye Sir.' They all replied in hushed tones.

'Right, now I want you to search for them through the shop, they'll be hidden somewhere amongst these font fronts no doubt. Off you go.'

A capital intervened and said 'Well I wouldn't go that way you know.'

'And why would you not be going that way Mr capital may I ask you?' asked Red with a fair bit of haughtiness in his tone.

'Well sir, the letters that have come with Stopper are rather well formed and will therefore be difficult to tell from the false font fronts at least from the front.'

'So you would suggest sir?'

'I'd suggest that the best way of finding the renegades is to look from the back seeing as how the false font fronts have only fronts then anything that has a back can't just be a front.'

'Capital suggestion sir, ok lads don't bother looking in front, our Mr Capital here has suggested such an approach would be a waste of time, so I suggest we concentrate on the backs.'

'Aye sir.'

All the letters went off on their search for the renegades.

All the letters in support of Stopper, except '*u*', for whom there were no false font fronts he could hide in front of, were well concealed right where they could be seen, without actually revealing themselves. Our highly strung '**f**' was buzzing with his sales pitch for high definition fonts with *u* as his less voluble assistant. Two of the Stopit gang were approaching them with some interest wondering why this '**f**' was still trying to sell when everyone else had gone.

'You're a bit late there my lower case friend are you not, there are no buyers here.'

Our salesman was unconcerned and gave them his finest pitch. 'HD Fonts, HD Fonts, get your HD Fonts right here, be seen from farther away, look better then you actually are, show the world an image that isn't you, enter the world of projection, fetch your wonderful inside out and the future is waiting for you.'

'HD?' one of the Stop-it two asked.

'Oh that's High Definition', his partner answered, 'although it's possible by the way he's talking there could be a reference to Humpty Dumpty in there too. That is one High Definition u there right enough. Is that font italicised f?'

'No Sir, he's just designed to please.'

'Very smart, almost real, but it's what you do with it, there's plenty of high def bullshit around wherever you look, and of course bullshit is bullshit whether it's high definition or invisible.'

'If you ask me the invisible stuff is more dangerous than the high def stuff, at least you can see the high def stuff.'

'Yes, but the high def font doesn't have a bullshit badge now does it, at least the barely visible has an excuse for not showing that it's bullshit, mind you I don't go with this constant pretence anyway I'm a staunch believer in fading with grace.'

'Yeah, I know what you mean, I'm getting tired of this city, seems to me that it's just like these fonts, all front, you know, funny though, when we were chasing those Stoppers, I felt a few of the letters around me more than I have for a long time, like we were just about to form some words, join up in meaning something, like we used to, that just doesn't happen here, it's beginning to seem to me that it isn't meant to happen.'

A comma hopped into view which gave our characters some pause, 'You must be with Red,' said the comma, and just before either of our two anonymous characters could muster forth a reply, the second comma hopped into view to add, 'which means you are with the Stop-Its,' and then, once again as they were about to reply, the final comma skipped into view to finish, 'and you want to make our Stopper stop.'

There was a gradual reassessment of the situation by the anonymous characters but they did manage to ask if 'one of you commas could shut the '**f**' up.' After a short space in letters they answered, 'to the first comma: yes, to the second: partly, and to the third: yes, they would like Stopper to stop, but for Stopper to stop when Stopper stopped.' This last part had a bit of a Humpty Dumpty feel to it.

The commas asked, 'which of them they would prefer to shut the '**f**' up, and would it not be better if they did it themselves?'

'Oh sorry, we thought you knew '**f**', which was why...'

'Perfectly understandable that you come in to a strange place, and I do believe this is a strange place for you, and you see a letter you don't know and then some commas you don't know, and then assume that the ones that you don't know must know each other, whereas the truth is that you two almost certainly know one another, we three know each other and judging by the way the '**f**' is talking in tautological loops, would suggest that he doesn't even know his self at the moment as it seems that tautological loops loop around the vocalist rather than through, but enough of this avoiding introductions. We are Alecto, Magaero, and Tisiphone, and we are the Erinyes, though sometimes we are the Euminides, and you are?'

'Well, we did arrive here in the company of Red and his cohorts but I wouldn't go so far as to say that we are exactly with Red, we were just kind of caught up in the commotion. We were actually on our way home when all this ripped through the street, we just got curious, got curious about this place too, not having been in here before, and now we're kind of curious about you too, seeing as we don't see many commas around here anymore.'

'Not even on your plates eh?'

'Pardon, we don't understand that.'

'Good that you don't, we can be Euminides then.'

'That's preferable to being Erinyes is it?'

'Oh yes, much, much, preferable, so much you wouldn't believe, let me put it this way you do not want to meet the Erinyes ever.'

Our two new characters, '**v**' and '**t**', to name them, being lower case letters were well aware of the rights and the powers of commas in sentences and were well aware that commas directions were important to observe correctly. Indeed they knew, as all lower case letters did, that the very word accommodating comes from the word comma as does accommodation as a place to rest. Capitals though had little contact with commas and were largely unaware of the need to accommodate them as were the even less knowledgeable numbers, and these two groups would likely feel the wrath of the Erinyes soon.

The commas, on their best Euminides behaviour, explained to 'v' and 't' that they also were anxious for Stopper to stop what was going on in Acronym City, in some ways even more so than they, then told these two that if Stopper was to stop the final sentence here in Acronym City then Acronym City would not only still be left standing but it would also mean that there were no alternative to this kind of place and system. They further added that they themselves would not allow Stopper to finish things here anyway, as they had already intimated to Stopper, they wanted the hell out of there as soon as possible, and that in fact was what they were currently trying to do. All in all they told the two letters it would be in their interests to help the Stoppers in thwarting the Stop-Its, or better still, if they could stop the Stop-It's from stopping Stopper, then they, meaning themselves, wouldn't have to stop here, and come to think of it, neither in the end would anyone else. So the 'v', the 't', the now quietened 'f', and the three commas were just about to go off in search of Stopper, when the recently called eager to please u revealed himself to be '*u*'.

The commas already were aware that Red and his cohorts were searching behind the False Font Fronts, so they led the letters right through the main parts of the shop so as to remain undisclosed. Red's cohorts in the meantime, searching fruitlessly for the Stoppers, were becoming extremely disturbed by a creeping feeling of utter emptiness. This was brought on by this constant looking behind these False Font Fronts. Few of the lower case letters had ever been in this shop other than the even fewer who were employed by capitals as assistants, so few of them had been in this shop before, and although most of them had seen False Font Fronts before, they had only seen them sporadically and more important in this particular case, only from the side that they should be seen from; the front. This sudden immersion amongst a great variety of these fronts seen from the side not to be shown to anything other than skin had a strangely negative effect on many of them.

Maybe it was the very fact that in a sense from the back these False Font Fronts were negative in a formal way in that they were the inverse of the natural form of the actual letter. Yet it seemed to be more than just a straight negative or opposite effect but something deeper, darker even. The backs of these False Fonts weren't the polished ink of the fronts but of a darkened hue with little or no concern for visual effect. What wasn't seen was not to be noticed was a kind of law of Acronym City, but it was a law that though rigidly followed, was somehow not itself noticed. Somehow the constant sight of the backs of these fonts brought that long unnoticed law to the front as it were. In a sense the backs of these fonts were representative of the lower case letters status in Acronym City.

Now many of these letters were with Red because they all felt that the situation in Acronym City was getting worse for them all the time and they wanted it to stop. It seemed they had some ill thought out ideas of somehow then reversing things in order to improve their own situations but many of these letters had been here so long that they had no knowledge of the extended empathetic proximity field and therefore had no thought of doing anything in order to recreate it, but worse than that they didn't realise that the very nature of Acronym City was built, indeed relied, on the decreasing conditions of the lower case letters status and general well being. Somehow this futile search of theirs was bearing fruit after all: it just wasn't what they were looking for; but it was what they needed to know.

Stopper was aware that all was not well in the ranks of the big Red, but Red was a charismatic leader, with his hungry look and piratical demeanour, who had been in Acronym City for a long time. Red had long realised that there was no hope for words and sentences in Acronym City, why, he said once to a friend, you could be talking about a completely different paragraph! Red had simply adapted to reality as he saw it. If meaning was meaningless, if Humpty Dumpty was the only semantic height to scale, then so be it. If single letters had to stand and be noticed then Red was up to it and he would do what was necessary in order to achieve this. Red of course was either unaware, or chose to be unaware, that the only reason he stood out was not because he was the letter r, nor even that he was a red font, no, the real reason he was able to stand up and have a hungry look and a piratical demeanour was simply because he was called Red, which involved the combination of three letters and a soupcon of semantic content, but as Red would have said himself, and often did, that was just such a different paragraph, maybe even a different chapter, and whatever semantic content managed to sneak through for Red, in this chapter, and in this paragraph he stood alone.

Oh well, alright, not quite alone, as he did in fact have a veritable host of disconsolate letters in his company.

The disconsolate letters were muttering now, at least that was what it sounded like to Stopper who was hiding in plain sight. It could be that what Stopper thought was muttering was just the sound of words not fully formed, as the individual letters of the search party passed by and disappeared into the darkness and silence from which they came. Stopper spotted the commas waiting at the end of the corridor, and so he sent out a whistle to the rest of his company, the sign they had agreed for them to reassemble and move on. As they all reassembled it seemed to Stopper that his group had grown somewhat even since entering this shop and he wasn't wrong. Many other letters had encountered old friends in the search group and like the commas, had convinced them to change sides. Once they had gathered together, leaving a few to look out for any of Red's party, they exchanged news of newcomers and got information from old comers. It seemed '**g**' had found the perfect place where they could hide and rest with complete peace and he was going to show them all the way. They went through the shop and found themselves in one of the numbers offices. They climbed up onto the desk and there they all saw the bottle waiting for them. One by one, they each of them climbed up the bottle and in they jumped... drip...drip...drip...drop...splash...splash...drip...drop...drip.

'So what was all the commotion last night then?' asked the exclamation mark on her way into the office of the False Font Front Shop. 'Would you look at this?' she cried and pointed down to this trail of ink that seemed to go from the door they had just entered through all the way to the ink bottle. 'This looks to me,' she said, in a somewhat peremptory manner 'that some messy writer borrowed this without asking and his or her inability to do things tidily has been revealed to us all, and doubtless this untidy individual will be revealed to us in time.'

In time leads us to Stopper with his rather bigger group of Stoppers as they seemed to be called, group wise at least, skirting through the back streets behind the shops. They had reasoned that as they would look extremely visible here they thought that Red probably wouldn't send anyone to look as he didn't fancy looking like a fool in front of the capitals and the numbers. Sending some of his troops off to the back of the shops would almost certainly generate some sarcastic remark from some smart assed capital and for Red such remarks were to be avoided at all costs. One of the Stop-its was telling Red that the Stoppers were nowhere to be found anywhere and he was tentatively suggesting that perhaps they should look at the back of the shops. Red got even redder than his normal shade, a rather nice burgundy actually, and admonished his letter severely, 'Search the back of the shops you imbecile, don't you think that would be a bit obvious?' Red was gratified to see cap C nod knowingly towards him which put Red at ease as it had been cap C who had pointed them to search at the backs of the fonts rather than the fronts. Red had merely used the same logic in his directions here and it seemed that in this at least cap C was a natural ally. Red never considered that in both uses of this particular species of logic no-one was to be discovered but as Red would say, and often did, that was just so last paragraph.

Speaking of last paragraphs, it seems that a hullabaloo had started in the False Font Front shop as the exclamation mark from that previous paragraph watched recently cleaned up ink spots begin to spontaneously reappear! The shrill shriek lanced its way through the aisles of the shop, right through the false fonts, shaking them violently as it passed and exploding out of both the front and back of the shop in between our two protagonists. At the sound of this shriek, both sets of letters, numbers and punctuation marks were galvanised into action as the ones at the front of the shop sped towards the back and the ones at the rear of the shop sped to the front, whilst in between some murmuring began yet not a word was spoken, at least not until both groups arrived in the vicinity of the exclaimer of that very shriek that had summoned them, at which point cries of astonishment rather than full formed words appeared to be the case.

Stopper and Red were standing opposite one another, but neither of them was aware of the other as their eyes were very much fixed on what was happening in between them. Before them were an exclamation mark and a question mark, who were deep in discussion. The exclamation mark had been explaining to the question mark that she had cleaned up the ink spots but when she came back had found that they had reappeared. She then cleaned them up and on returning a little later had found them back again. Growing increasingly concerned about her own perception, not to mention her sanity, she had hurriedly cleaned the ink spots up again. This time though, she stayed to watch and as she stood there doubting her own reason, she saw the ink spots come back spontaneously and that was when she screamed.

She had just cleaned them up again so everyone could see, and sure as her own sanity back they came. Still, they spooked her nonetheless, so that she felt a compulsion to immediately clean them up. Stopper, having spoken to '*u*' and the commas, asked her to leave them the next time they came back as he felt sure that they had started to move just as she cleaned them up. They watched as once again the ink spots came back, but this time no-one cleaned them up, although the exclamation mark had to stop herself from doing so, and before long it became apparent that the ink spots were moving. They began to move and space out to either side and then other ink spots appeared to replace the ones that moved out and then they did the same until they themselves were replaced. Eventually they had formed the shape of a circle and then the ink spots began to merge to complete the circle, then the circle began to rise up from the floor which elicited an audible collective gasp from the onlookers as the circle, shimmering now stood vertical before them. A ghostly voice came from the circle now that asked if Stopper was present. Stopper stepped forward and answered yes and was beckoned to enter the shimmering circle, just before he entered he turned and nodded to the commas whereupon the commas positioned themselves at the optimum defensive points should there be any kind of advance from Red whilst Stopper was gone. Stopper then told '*u*' he would be back as soon as he could and that they should make ready to dash for the Ink Well as soon as he returned and with that Stopper stepped into the circle and disappeared.

'Well, quite an entrance, I must say, I love that shimmering dress, when did you get that one?'

'Stopper, will you behave, this is no time for frivolity!'

'Frivolity, Zero my dear, there is nothing frivolous about, either my attitude towards, nor my desire for you my most fulsome emptiness, you virtual tease you, come here.'

'I'm already 'here' as you know well, so when are you leaving here?'

'Were just about to, if we can get away from Red and the Stop-it's that is.'

'Red; that must be the one on the other side of me is it?'

Stopper explained to Zero of Reds leadership and demeanour and Zero nodded as she gathered the picture of the situation. 'You could say,' Zero opined, 'that there's nothing between you seeing as he's just leading them because he can, and because he stands out more than the others.'

'Yes, that's what I've been informed, he's not really interested in what they want, in fact he personally, as a letter that is, wouldn't want Acronym City to fall, being red he'd never get jobs in words, they wouldn't put up with it would they, letters outshining words, that would be semantic stupidity.'

'Acronym City appears to be somewhat bereft of words anyway, I guess that's why he's so popular.'

'It certainly helps, and he has certainly adapted very well, of course he may want to really capture me and make me finish everything because he actually agrees with me about what that would actually do.'

Which is?'

'If I were to stop the few sentences left here we would all be left here, everyone would be left here forever: there wouldn't be any way out. Acronym City would be the great shining city on the hill but its light would only be for itself.'

'I'm inclined to agree. So you best make sure you get over here, there are a lot of words and sentences waiting to meet you.'

They, and you, shall have to wait, I'll have to go now, and I have a hunch I've got some commas to control.'

'Well when you return they will be able to control things again.'

'I'm talking control of an extremely harsh nature,' and he told her about the deep fried commas tails and how they had vowed revenge against the capitals and the numbers. 'They've got a particular fate in store for Cap C.'

'Cap C, Stopper, no, he's on our side!

'On our side you say? Well, well, funny, I never thought of him as an enemy, he was never all the way with the more vertical capitals, must have been his big curvaceous nature eh?'

'You best get back and stop the commas doing something they'll regret, we can't have misplaced commas at this stage Stopper; go!'

Stopper reappeared returning out of the shimmering blue ring which slowly lost its' shimmer, its' verticality and its' very substance. The exclamation mark exclaimed that she didn't even need to clean the ink spots up; they were just gone, as if by magic. It was almost as if nothing was there. The poor shaken exclamation mark felt completely bereft of purpose at this point, her purpose being to clean those damned ink stops. No more 'Out, out, damned ink spots' from her

Stopper stepped out just in time to see the commas approaching the numbers and capitals who had arrived whilst Stopper was gone. As Stopper started towards them he saw these small fun-filled punctuation marks make their mark in front of the numbers and capitals, but numbers weren't of a nature to pause other than to compare and the capitals had little contact with commas even back in more wordy days. So, none of the numbers or capitals heeded the commas in front of them and their lack of attention. It was said later that they must have been so over confident that they were actually close to being comatose not to have seen the transformation of the commas until it was too late.

Now although everyone who witnessed this could, and did in fact, swear that the commas grew monstrous in their transformation, they didn't actually get any bigger at all. What they did is raise their resolution, in more ways than one it should be added, to such an extent that not only were they completely determined to exact some revenge for the deep fried commas tails, but that they were screwed up to such a high definition that they were no longer seen as the small well defined curvaceous printed characters they normally were, but at this level of HD they looked as though they had been painted by some demented child, such that the curves were lost amongst the accoutrements they now appeared to sport, with numerous unattractive phantasmagorical protuberances with seemingly no purpose but to stir the imagination in too much to imagine kind of ways. This high definition gave the commas a lumbering slow look, yet they retained all of their usual agility, and it was this that enabled them to attack with some abandon, which they promptly did. In motion they were still basically curvaceous, but once there, facing their chosen opponents, they were a horror to behold. They would spring from their tails and land in front of their prey and at each spring they would each of them scream one letter, one would scream C, the next would scream G, and finally, the third would scream I: CGI. This it turns out stood for Commas Going In, but it certainly kept many a lower case letter animated for some considerable time.

These attacks had a devastating effect on the numbers and capitals, what with the numbers being the supremely smooth operators they had become they could not handle these HD commas and their rough looks and behaviour, and as for the capitals they had been so aloof from all other letter considerations that prior to the close sense of acronymic brotherhood that had briefly held sway for a while back when Acronym City was being constructed, they had only looked at other capitals from a distance but most of the time they had simply stared into space, which could account for rather a lot of things, what with nature abhorring a vacuum and the like. So the commas were sending the numbers and the capitals reeling and as they made their way through the throng as it were, it being less of a throng by the time they were finished, they, all three of them, spotted Cap C looking a little perturbed at proceedings and just as all three commas sprang to land directly in front of Cap C they found themselves facing a completely impassable full stop: Stopper had intervened.

Whilst Stopper had been away and the commas had transformed themselves one of the effects of this vendetta of the commas was to inspire a mix of fear and envy in Red and his troops. After all, although Red had adapted to Acronym City as best he could, he was still aware that things were far from right in this city and the characters most responsible for that lack of rightness were the very characters being slaughtered by the fury bent commas. So Red didn't know whether he should try and defend the numbers and capitals, or at least make out as if he was going to, seeing as actually defending anyone against this onslaught of the commas was not an option worth a red fonted r's tip of the tongue as it were, or whether he should, right now a much safer option, quietly support the commas. The second option was in fact the only default option under the circumstances but Red was aware that he'd best be a little circumspect regarding that quiet, bordering on silence, if truth be told, support. Add to this the fact that Red and quite a few of his troops had been awe struck by Zero's shimmering circle so being more than a little circumspect under the circumstances was completely understandable.

So as Stopper stopped the commas from their destructive drive to make capitals and numbers pause for a very, very long time, by quietly reminding them that that was the job of semi colons and colons, Red had been busy doing nothing whilst admiring nothing and hesitating to release himself and his friends from their self imposed long pause. So despite three rampaging furies and a shimmering blue circle, the disappearance of Stopper and his subsequence reappearance, Stopper and Red were still facing one another as if nothing had happened, which in one way at least was quite true, but now there was nothing to stop them confronting one another, or at least that was how Red saw things as the numbers and the capitals were gathering round again and Red knew his moment was come.

'Stopper,' Red cried, 'I hear tell you're about to be vacating this City! Now, far be it from me to prevent the sick, the poor, and the mildly brain addled from leaving this City, but I believe you are looking to leave here with some of my letters in tow and that you have some information that would be of some benefit to us. How say you Stopper?'

Red puffed himself up to his most important size; no need of false font fronts here, Red was one fine looking r if ever there was such a thing. Stopper, who was on the point of turning away, reluctantly turned back to face his accuser, and waiting a little for the commas to flank him he eyed, not Red himself, but the capitals and numbers who had now regrouped, at least the ones that still could after the assault of the commas. All in all there were a lot more numbers and letters on Red's side than there were on Stopper's but neither capitals nor numbers were familiar with punctuation marks in any other way than as servants in the shops and institutions of Acronym City, so, they had no idea whatever about punctuation independence, indeed, they had always considered punctuation marks to be dependent on them, which, prior to the onslaught of the furies was how things were; so, they weren't aware of it as yet, but the rules of Acronym City were changing.

Prior to this point rules were walls that held in the lower case letters and punctuation marks, and these rules had to be observed by those self same characters. They could find ways to break some rules but it was like as if they'd actually climbed a wall so there was another wall beyond that one. It didn't matter what you did, you could climb, get round, get over, burrow under, skip through, but you could never get beyond these rules. Now that may seem reasonable for letters and punctuation marks, there being a need for rules to generate words and sentences with any kind of semantic information, but here in Acronym City there were no words or sentences to speak of, these were rules not to produce anything at all, rules, in fact that simply generated rules. They even invented a word to explain this system. They called it iteration, which was the act of producing another it. It doesn't matter what it is as long as it is, and if it is it then we have iteration! The capitals and numbers of course held themselves to be beyond these rules, beyond the walls as it were, and so these rules never changed in any way but additively, a rather tiresome habit of the numbers that when added to the iteration process produced multiplication, and this was what fed the constant generation of rules that the capitals put up with just to make themselves look busy and self important, and if there's one thing that capitals were always absolutely brilliant at it was their wonderfully over the top, or wall if you like, sense of self importance.

So, Stopper looked out at a preening piratical red fonted r, flanked by a host of faded lower case letters who were definitely wavering, either in their support or actually in reality, which ever they were not really any kind of threat. There were still a load of self important capitals to consider but Stopper was fairly sure that the capitals sense of self importance would result in them keeping themselves well out of harm's way. As for the numbers Stopper wasn't sure what they would do but what he did know was that whereas in the past they may well have resorted to the art of division and subtraction to tackle Stopper with, they were now so wrapped up in vociferous agreement productivity terms that they could only add and multiply. Stopper knew that this constant addition and multiplication and the constant use of comparisons, less thans, and more thans modifiers were completely neglecting any uses of equals signs. Indeed it was some wag of a number who had said, 'It depends what the definition of is, is.' This coupled with the use of iteration transferred the numbers focus from the is to the it and with them being completely unconcerned about what the it actually was the overall effect was that all contact with reality, truth and of any semantic understanding were going the same way as the equals sign, their use diminishing to Zero. In effect the numbers didn't care, and this along with their ever increasing closeness to even the concept of Zero was beginning to piss Stopper off. On top of that this lot had been Humpty Dumpty'd to Hell who said what they meant and meant what they said, a verbal iterative process if ever there was, whilst Stopper and his group of friends still said what they meant because they knew that it actually meant something, and they often said things they didn't actually mean, not because they didn't care but because they actually did. So Stopper at last brought his gaze back to Red and was ready to answer him with what he fervently hoped would be wit, wisdom and wordiness. It was nearing time to put letters back in their place; the words were waiting, with bated breath, for a voice.

'Ah Red, you look fine and handsome in your deep dark red finery there, but your brothers, they are fading and tattered and worn. There are ghosts all around us now Red, shimmering spaces that make it look like the letters are moving, but it's all an illusion Red, nothing is moving, nothing but ghosts on this page. When you lock down your letters and you don't permit free words, when you abbreviate short sentences to short gaps that would rather be filled, and the acronym means more than what's voiced, what do we do with the ghosts on the page, Red? They were looking for words and sentences to die for Red, not words and sentences to die in. These letters don't move, Red, words within sentences can, but not on this page, Red, not on this page. There are ghosts all around us Red, phantoms unseen. Red I'm not taking any of your letters anywhere, they are leaving this city of their own accord, ah yes, I hear you say, they would never leave were you not here; they only follow you. No Red, they only leave because there's nothing more for them here Red, the future left here some time ago, it scurried unseen up the hill you know as Avoidance Avenue, the future still here is a phantom Red, a phantom that's locked in the past. These ghosts are not accidents Red, none of them are, and neither are they to do with the scream of the Amygdala, though perhaps that's not quite true, but no, they are part of the city's manufacturing process, a waste product produced to make Humpty Dumpty paste, a product that lets you speak nonsense with confidence for the price of a ghost Red, that's what they are leaving, that's why they are leaving. Soon there will be more ghosts than characters, who will you help then Red, for the cost of Humpty Dumpty will rise as it's useless effects fail and then you'll be alone Red, none to empathise with, none to be near and nowhere to extend, words will fail you as the only things left here are Acronyms none understand in this semantic free Zone. Come with us Red, there's nothing left here, no-one to aid.'

'There are ghosts.' Red replied and striding towards the three big capitals at the top of the hill, he paused and turned and looking towards the commas, cried 'CGI,' and the commas grew and leapt in and landing in front of these capitals ripped off their false font fronts to reveal what remained of the capitals. They were clothed in cassocks and cowls that had cloth that shimmered darkly, a dull sheen as of snakeskin. The dark maw of the hood showed nothing inside, and a gasp went up from the letters nearby and grew louder for they'd seen what none had ever guessed.

The capitals were completely wrapped in numbers.

END OF PART TWO

SECOND INTERLUDE

Red and Stopper were talking by the bracket past the Ink Well. All the other letters that had come with Stopper, and the commas of course, plus the letters that had since joined them were readying for their trip through the unconscious.

'They can't make it through the unconscious, there's nothing to hold them together in there, they're stuck here Red.' Stopper was speaking of the ghosts; there was no way through for them. Red, who was staying behind promised to look after them, promised to do what he could for them. He had some letters who were staying with him, plus there were still many letters and punctuation marks in Acronym City who had had nothing to do with recent events. Acronym City would still be producing ghosts. The commas thought the city's supply of letters was assured by the probable continuing raids on the subconscious they'd come from. Few letters, never mind ghosts, once they'd gone, they thought ruefully, would leave Acronym City.

Stopper was ready to go but he would pass the bracket last on the way in. The commas went in just before him knowing their high resolution gymnastics would be unavailable to them once in here, so they entered the unconscious with an air of trepidation, not that any of the others felt much better. The unconscious is not a good environment for the virtuals, there is no supporting environment, so only well formed letters, numbers and punctuation marks could hold themselves together in there. Words could not hold together at all, there being no extended empathetic proximity field in the unconscious to give them meaning, which is why of course, no messages or essentially two dimensional information can be passed through. Numbers had the least trouble as they always referred to something else so they had no meaning as such to hold on to in the first place. This time though they would not have to encounter the scream of the Amygdala, but they would have to go the way of the Hypothalamus. Stopper had earlier explained that where the Amygdala's creative memory of their earlier encounter would have prepared the Hypothalamus for the one to come and that this would be a gentler encounter but with further consequences than before. So, care had to be taken as they descended the neural pathways through the dendrite trees down and down and down to the Hypothalamus.

As they approached the area near the Hypothalamus Stopper told them in hushed tones not to disturb anything around there as they did not want to cause any rage to emanate from the Hypothalamus what with the potential repercussions involved, although he did indicate again that their previous visit to the Amygdala would hopefully make the Hypothalamus consider them as a part of the environment rather than the aliens that they were. As '*u*' put it, we don't want a psycho Hypo. As they drew closer they could hear a kind of murmur or maybe it was more of a grumbling from down below.

The murmur or grumbling sound, well no, sound wasn't the thing here, just as the last trip in the unconscious it was more as if the environment told you that, that the sense of murmuring or grumbling enveloped you, went through you, soaked you through. Down here you could not, not, know. Denial was not an option. Anyway they had managed to get around half of them past the Hypothalamus when Hypo let them know he knew they were there.

'So just where do you think you lot are going?' he soaked them, as it were.

'Oops,' kind of permeated their being at that point, or those points perhaps would be better. 'Oops was no longer a two dimensional line read from left to right over time, the letters felt washed in 'oopness' or like a wind of 'oopness' blew through them, it's presence could not be denied and neither could what followed. In a way it was like a strange version of the semantic field they generated in words and sentences, but this emanated from everywhere it seemed.

'Oops isn't really a reply you know, it's one of those words you lot come up with to bridge semantic valleys, something to get you from one meaning to the next without losing understanding, most of you letters will end up like that you know, bridging gaps between meanings.'

'Well thanks for your moral appraisal', said 'g', 'I'm sure we'll benefit greatly from your good words.'

'First of all I don't use words, you do, and as you do, you perceive words. You take meaning in full flight and you roll it up into words and then putting words together you re release it and then you congratulate yourselves on your creativity. You take a free flying gas, liquidise it and then leave it to evaporate and call it literature when all it is, is wind, it's just been redirected.'

'For one who doesn't use words you've no shortage of opinions on them have you?'

'Ah Stopper, you've arrived eh? Welcome to the reality beneath the imagination.'

'That's a bit of a grand claim isn't it?'

'It certainly is, and I could not claim anything less given my position, authority, connections and control.'

'Did you forget freakery there?' Now '*u*' didn't mean to say that out loud, indeed he didn't think he did, but communication in the unconscious was kind of uncontrollable, which given *u*'s inadvertent, no, not inadvertent at all, but more, rather uncontrolled, comment from before, was a tad ironic.

'No, I didn't, I just left it to you, or is that '*u*'?'

Stopper was almost envious of that one. 'So you have control then?'

'Yep.'

'So, how does that work, and how do you understand meaning?'

'Chemistry, my dear boy; chemistry. Chemical fields, chemical potentials, chemical interfaces, chemical barriers, chemical gates, chemical concentrations, chemical eddies, chemical flow. Stopper, with chemical connections they're felt, they're smelt, they're touched, and they sometimes get in your throat, but they are always there and they can't be denied. The closest you and your ilk get is ink.'

'Maybe your right, but I didn't know that communication and understanding were meant to be competitive!'

'Stopper, you've just come from Acronym City, how can you say that semantic understanding isn't competitive?'

'Well, back there, they're just trying to close down understanding.'

'Hey Hypo, we got a dopamine delivery to go, everything ok?'

'Yeah, hang on a mo, sorry Stopper, busy, busy, busy.'

'Ok we can wait but not too long.'

'I thought you were smart Stopper, sure they're closing it down but that's not the end of it, the point is to control understanding so they don't have to worry about anything breaking out or in. The entire city is built on lies of agreement, Stopper, the kind of things that used to be called gentlemen's agreements in the sense that the gentleman might well be lying through his carefully kept teeth, but he would still be a gentleman, and it was in fact the agreement to be a gentleman that they agreed upon, and nothing else. Now though, they've long agreed to agree only on the agreeable, what is deemed agreeable to these egregious agreeing agreeable twats is that the disagreeable being visited on those who remain disagreeable to these mendacious agreements are deemed enemies of the great agreement, and thereby supremely disagreeable to such an extent that they need their disagreeable tendencies curtailed.'

'I'm usually smarter at the end of a sentence as it happens but I'm not completely clear in this chemical environment where the sentence ends.'

'Oh sentences don't end here Stopper, they just kind of linger and then they gradually fade away. You'll probably be aware of a kind of mounting slightly changing repetition effect in the way you perceive what the chemicals are telling me, that's just the way you can understand it. It's not the way I understand it. You virtuals are rather limited when it gets right down to it Stopper, but then again it's those very limits that give you your liberty to speak.'

'Serotonin delivery been blocked by oxytocin going out Hypo.'

'Ok let the o out then the s in, hmm, these letters must be affecting me!'

'So you won't mind if I speak my mind then?'

'Not at all, and I see you're catching on to the repetition trick.'

'Yes, well, it wasn't quite meant that way.'

'Oh it was Stopper, it was.'

'The Amygdala indicated, that, although the chemicals themselves cannot lie, that nevertheless the producer of the chemical flow could have untruthful intention behind that production in the first place.'

'Sounds like the production process of Humpty Dumpty paste there, Stopper, but the Amygdala doesn't have the connections that I have which leaves room for some doubt on the part of the Amygdala which is as things should be. See, the Amygdala has to be in a state of readiness to impart critical information, to be honest this state of readiness means he doesn't actually do much most of the time, bugger all comes to mind, so this constant state of alertness makes my old friend somewhat doubtful, this has always been the problem with security work, me, myself, am just busy all the time, doing things to keep things going and in order to function means having to trust the information coming my way.'

'So the Amygdala has to be sceptical but you have to be credulous?'

'That's about the size of it Stopper, the way it works my little rotund friend.'

'So what if the Amygdala is right in his sceptical outlook but you're wrong in your trust?'

'You mean that I'm being lied to?'

'Yes.'

'Well I wouldn't know about that, but you might, then again the Amygdala would warn me but of course I'd likely put that down to being due to the fear of the Amygdala rather than anything real, unless it kept going.'

'Well, hasn't the Amygdala been screaming for some time now?'

'Yes he has as it happens and I am aware of it.'

'Which means?'

'Which means I'm looking into it, trying to fix it, could you excuse me a moment I've got a message to send to the Pituitary Gland?'

'Does repetition have a role in that fixing by any chance?'

'Well yes it does, hang on a minute...ACTH, yes send it down to the pit, oh and a little TSH if there's any left.'

'Syntax sakes,' thought '*u*', 'we got acronyms and repetition down here.'

'Yes, I thought as much, you see, repetition is at the heart of the problem in the language system, it's made small talk micro talk, and it's made small minds micro minds, as they repeat ad infinitum whatever they're fed with not only no check on verifiability but with a need for no verifiability to begin with so as to enhance non-falsifiability which itself allows them to, as you put it so well before, lie through their well kept teeth.'

'So you're suggesting that my repeated attempts to repair a real problem that I've been informed of by the Amygdala is itself creating a problem in the virtual system of language and that that problem in the virtual world is looping back to cause the problem I'm trying to fix in this real world.'

'I couldn't have put it better myself.'

'Correct, you didn't.'

'No wonder the Amygdala screams.'

'I caught that you commas.'

'We were just appraising the general malaise of the current real and virtual situations and merely noting the strain this is likely to put on the rather put on Amygdala, oh look at that, repetition can be fun!', rejoined the commas.

'Hmm, looks like you three can do your resolution tricks down here after all.'

'Ah well now, repetition is more or less, mostly more in fact, the way things are done here, not by choice but just by the way things are here. At the fundamental level we have repeated pulses of electrical activity travelling along the axons to the neurons and if there is enough repetition this closes the synapse on that neuron which then sends another signal along another axon. So a message is generated – whoosh – along the axon –whoosh – goes another and – whoosh – goes another one and then you get a push on the synapse and a new message goes– whoosh – then another goes – whoosh – and then – whoosh – and then push. This activity is repeated in what is a 4 dimensional syncopated dance that is repeated and repeated and repeated until the activity affects the chemical potentials which is where I come in. I monitor and control the flow of chemicals around the main parts of the brain that keep it working well. There is only so much you can do as regards chemical and much of that depends on your equipment. I have adequate equipment but in the end much of what I then do is by its nature rather repetitive. So yes, there certainly is a lot, a Hell of a lot in fact, repetition down here, but the whole point of the repetition is that with what is basically a cumulative system then that repetition is absolutely essential to take it to next stage and the next stage and the next stage after that until from the cumulative rhythms and patterns comes the open pages above that lets this beast know it exists.'

'So down here you need a lot of repetition to get things going to make things happen, whereas up there too much repetition gets tedious, numbing, too little down here does nothing, sparingly used up there it is most effective. Interesting but we can't, like sentences here, linger much longer, much though I'd like to continue this communication.'

Well, I'm far too busy anyway, and as you say you best be on your way. Look out for Misery by the way.'

'Misery? I've seen too much of that in Acronym City.'

No, Stopper, those were the effects of Misery, not Misery herself, you must speak with her.'

The company set off again and as they left the Hypothalamus the descent got deeper and steeper than before and our letters now had to tread carefully, a fallen letter here could get mixed up in one of the acronyms and then no-one would know what it meant! Now wouldn't that be tragic? At last they saw the second bracket ahead and they finally arose from the unconscious back into the virtual world of the imagination, or so they imagined. Zero awaited Stopper and wilfully, wishfully, whisked him away...

PART THREE

The three commas were skipping and chatting their way down Conversation Avenue heading for Verbals where they were hoping to get some news of Stopper, his whereabouts, though that wasn't too difficult to guess, his state of health, and last but not least, his intentions. The commas still were somewhat abashed at their high resolution antics in Acronym City, after all they hadn't expected any such thing, hadn't planned it, or set out any kind of strategy, they just did it. They were still abashed but also more than a little bit awed at what they'd done back there, but it was what they had seen at the Humpty Dumpty factory that had done it, they thought. They may not have Stoppers sense of understanding at the end of things but they certainly could see the way things were going from their perspectives and they did not like the direction taken in Acronym City. As far as they were concerned Acronym City was an abomination and the capitals were to blame for it, only capitals could treat ghosts worse than if they weren't there whilst keeping then on the edge of non existence for as long as their phantom existence was profitable. It was obscene! They were still miffed at not being allowed to take out Cap C, and they were more than a little miffed at Cap C coming through here with them. So they'd been keeping tabs on the captain and following him in three shifts, one comma at a time; that would give him pause. Today though, they'd given the captain free rein as they'd decided to get together again and catch up with one another, and hopefully with the others they'd been adventuring with, for what seemed to them now, an awful lot of paragraphs ago.

As they entered Verbals, they saw 's', the italicised '*u*', and the '**i**', waiting for them, 'Oh yes, what's this then; a pairing off situation? We know your number you know.'

The '**s**' looked decidedly slippery, the '*u*' looked set to run away, and the '**i**' almost lost his hat in his haste to compose his lower self in a less than unseemly manner. 'Oh settle down,' they said, 'now who's buying?'

After a short space of small talk they found they felt an aversion to talking of Acronym City, a need, in fact to avoid the memory, which was strange given that that was where their most memorable recent experiences were. Even more odd was the fact that they all wanted to talk of the experience of the Hypothalamus, but they could not remember anything worthwhile to relate. A clear case it seems of wanting to discuss the stuff they could not understand rather than the stuff they thought they understood too well, which, of course they'd have to discuss sooner or later, but for now, deference was their definite preference. So they fell into a rather languorous talk peppered with pregnant pauses and post haste retorts which carried on until the unforgotten feel of Avoidance Avenue began to reassert itself on the company, like some dark uninvited character who had arrived at the next table to them who was paying much too much attention to their gathering. The compulsion to recall aloud their blasted and emotional scars from their recent experience became too much to hold back and so the inkwells opened and gushed their contents over their wasted wants to retain any measure of decorum, like a spontaneous Rorschach test that shows your state of mind.

One thing was for sure, none of them liked that place at all, they didn't understand it nor want to really, but seeing what was under every representation, every syllable, every single good sounding thing, the extent of misery and semantic loss was palpable in its anguish. They didn't fully understand what that semantic loss really meant in the way Stopper did but they knew enough to know enough, and that was enough for now. The commas spoke about the Humpty Dumpty factory and the ghosts and the shortness of the sentences, the way the same thing was said again and again and again until it lost any meaning it first had anyway. The loss of meaning, they said, was only partly due to repetition, the other part of that loss was the lack of any other sentences or utterances to compare, enlarge, or comment, on the first, so this constant repetition led directly to loss of reciprocation. So rather than the repetition itself, or perhaps that should be selves, being responsible for the semantic loss, it is, in fact the intention behind the repetition in the first place that is the primary cause of the semantic holes in the vacuous talk that stands for discourse in Acronym City. The others gazed at the commas in yet more admiration, in addition to the previous admiration for their recent Furies incarnation, as they explained this, whilst '*u*' passed the quiet opinion that they had been fraternising with Stopper for a bit too long by the sound of it, 'unlike '*u*' of course,' said Stopper who had quietly rolled in to join the present company.

The commas quickly started firing questions at him but he just as quickly shushed them down as he gestured towards the other letters and began to talk small talk to them to take all the tension and any sense of urgency out of the atmosphere. It was time for calmness and cool, and also time to get beyond Acronym City in their minds. They had to find some way of remembering what happened with the Hypothalamus, Stopper had tried to remember, with Zero goading him, pulling him, pushing him, but all to no avail, and none of the others had been able to remember anything from there either, which was why, mentally they were all still stuck in Acronym City. Acronym City was the kind of place that simply didn't let go, and although, Stopper thought, maybe it shouldn't really, there was a need to address the Hypothalamus episode in order to move on, for moving on was necessary for his ongoing investigations.

'Well my little Furies,' Stopper said to the commas, 'which of you is Alecto, which of you Magaero, and which of you is Tisiphone then?' Each comma nodded acquiescence at their prompted names in turn, settling the question in three simple nods and a triple flick of the tail.

'Now I'd like to speak of your stint as Furies but we need to get to grips with the Hypothalamus experience.'

'Well, that's a good seeming idea but none of us can remember anything about it.'

'Talking about stuff you can't remember, isn't that called psychotherapy?'

'Not in this case it isn't, the reason we can't remember anything from there is simply because our means of communication and remembrance don't work in that particular environment and so trying to remember in the normal way isn't going to work, try as we might, so we have to find other ways, more feeling than thinking ways to bring some aspects of it back into our own system where we can rebuild it and then remember it.'

'Still sounds like psychotherapy to me.' '*u*' added.

'I see you've got your ink levels back to black,' Stopper replied.

'Yes, and I see you've got your density back too,' countered '*u*'.

The commas giggled a little at that and Stopper glared as only full stops can to arrest their wan but wanton laughter.

'Oh leave them alone Stopper,' said '**i**', 'they haven't had much to laugh about lately.'

'Well they've plenty to be happy about haven't they? They're out of Acronym City; they're in the big town of words where they can participate in the temporary sentences and where you letters can enter the word exchange.'

'Oh yes,' replied '*u*', 'we were having a conversation about that just before the commas arrived and interrupted our sentences, we're going in there tomorrow.'

'Hmmph!, replied the commas, deliberately using a word without vowels to show their discontent with the letters in their company, 'we only gave you pause, that is not', and here they paused for effect, 'an interruption.'

'Do you think we could interrupt this argument and join you?' called '**s**' and '**t**' who had just arrived in the midst of this.

'It is not an argument!' replied '*u*'.

'No', Stopper agreed, 'just a fairly forcible syntactical discussion.'

The commas, despite their contribution to this 'syntactical discussion', or even despite themselves, could not help but laugh at Stoppers interjection, and, when Stopper looked back, felt the need to curl up in some embarrassment, but no shame. As a number of es quietly arrived they unfurled their collective embarrassment back to their natural curvature.

'Well, seems to me there are enough of us here to try and figure out where we go from here.' Stopper announced.

'We could do with numbers if we want to figure anything.' Said the 't'. 'Hmm, 'i', you're always fraternising with numbers, do you think you could get some to come along?'

The 'i' was beside himself with anger at this accusation and denied it vociferously only for the other' 'i to admit it freely, which was the usual downside to getting beside yourself in anger, grief, or any other highly charged emotional state you care to mention. Truth will out but only after the lie, its essence usually somewhere in between the two. Like the double affirmative of Aye-aye, the first has a full positive affirmation whereas the second, in seeming support of the first, actually subverts it by allowing in some doubt; hyphens don't join things, they keep them apart. Speaking of which, a hyphen actually joined the company at that juncture in the proceedings, join here being on a different part of the semantic slope from the aforementioned join of course. Finally Zero and 8 arrived and everyone settled down to discuss their situation.

Across the way, in Buzzwords, were a group of words observing this motley crew of loose letters, numbers, and punctuation marks, in some consternation it must be said, as loose letters were something of a rarity in this paragraph at least. So far though, the words kept themselves to themselves, as they were not yet of a mind to spread their semantic largesse beyond themselves at this point in the proceedings, preferring instead to await sufficient semantic pregnancy prior to voicing their growing concerns. Loose letters in the world of words, whoever heard of such a thing? A few of the words were worried that this incursion of letters was a clandestine attack of acronyms, after all, hadn't they just come from Acronym City? The presence of the commas and the full stop calmed their fears down but the basic suspicion didn't entirely go away.

Some of the words were amazed at the communication skills of these loose letters and unsentenced punctuation marks for any words exchanged between the letters were longer than the speakers themselves and for the commas and full stop they weren't just longer but bigger too and that was impressive! There were certain effects caused by this length and size discrepancy of course, one of which was a noticeable increase in the levels of repetition in their discourse due to the fact that words being longer than the speaker are apt to be forgotten more often than not. Indeed, little known now is the fact that it was the letters that wanted to develop the art of writing rather than the words themselves, who were happy just to have voice. The letters had of course evolved this way and part of the drive to join words came from this need to remember, but you can't have all the letters used up in words or you wouldn't be able to make up new words, not to mention the difficulties of playing scrabble without loose letters. So from the combination of the letters proneness to forgetting what they'd just said and from the need for forgetful letters to feed the words to come the lower case letters began to relate to the punctuation marks in order to jog, as it were, their memories. If they needed to know what was about to happen, or where the speech was heading they would consult the colon and the semi-colon. If they wanted to know what was going on at the time, or what the current situation was they would consult the commas, and if they wanted to know what had happened, or what it all meant, they consulted the full stop. You could say that the colons had foresight, the commas eyesight, and the full stop hindsight. So this combination of talents enabled the loose letters to gain some understanding of what was going on.

This worked reasonably well but they still needed much repetition, and in order to reach beyond the current sentence the letters developed the art of writing, a technique which would lead to permanence of memory. Back in the day, the lower case letters also consulted the capitals as well as the colons for their apparent talents of foresight. In time of course they realised that the capitals rather than having foresight, had an agenda, which they disguised as foresight, thereby creating an accumulation of self fulfilling prophecies.

So it was the letters that led to writing, for it is remembered in the language itself; that writers were formerly known as men of letters; to speak and write properly was to mind your ps and qs. Higher education brought letters after your name, though it must be said that this was the first step onto the semantic slope to acronymic contraction, but these first steps were innocently taken for the right reasons. So it was the letters and the punctuation marks that pushed for writing to begin with. This push from the letters annoyed the words, who were taken to speaking their minds on this subject and swiftly fell into the oral history camp in staunch opposition to these scribes. The words held Homer to be of their camp whilst the letters claimed Plato to be of theirs. Strange to say is that by all accounts Homer used repetition in the same way as letters did in order to aid memory, so in many ways Homer was actually in the letters camp, possibly for the same reason; both being pre-writing. The word scribes is interesting in this tale because it too is a first step towards acronymic contraction for not so innocent reasons this time because scribes is an abbreviation of describes and was meant as an insult in that the scribes couldn't describe without marks and marks on scrolls of papyrus and reams of paper. So words had always been wary of letters, and somewhat suspicious of punctuation marks.

The words were particularly worried to see the s amongst the letters with his slideability and pluralisation skills, this reminded the words of the tragic tale of the word inane. It seems the word inane in a bit of a mix up of semantic levels became convinced that his meaning of meaninglessness applied to his self too, so the word inane thought not only did he mean meaningless, but that he was therefore meaningless, so, over time inane got depressed about this awful situation. Consulting his aunt inanity they decided that they would court the letter '**s**' and use pluralisation as a route to re-establishing meaning in their lives. So inane became inanes but still meaning didn't seem to confer itself upon the inanes. In the end there were so many inanes that meaning simply fled the area at which point all of the s's decided they would be better off behind the first n, where they would re-establish meaning and be more truthful to boot: all of the inanes turned insane. So the words did not like loose letters around at all, they could cause all sorts of mischief. Whereas, they weren't worried at all about the punctuation marks but then they didn't know of the furies, and of Stopper they knew nothing at all.

Our heroes of course were unaware of the wariness of words to them and were in a more precarious position than they realised. As far as they were concerned being out of Acronym City was victory itself, and being beyond the clutches of the stop-its was, as some of them were trying to sway things this way, cause for celebration. Stopper wasn't about to let them celebrate anything, he knew they were still in a precarious position, he knew they would have to get the words on their side, he knew that the capitals here could still cause them problems and he also was sure, though he'd no idea how, that he hadn't seen the last of the stop-its, much though he hoped that he had. Also the commas were more aware than Stopper gave them credit for, this giggling gaggle of commas were much changed since their recent experiences and were more aware of the wariness of the words than Stopper was for one. Be that as it may, they had many sheets of paper to cross yet, much ink to be consumed in that endeavour.

So again they were trying to find a way back to the experience of the hypothalamus with a singular, no, make that multiple, lack of success, when '*u*' once again suggested that this was looking more like a psychotherapy session rather than a syntactical session. The s then rounded on him accusing him of closing down arguments using repetition which was the same technique practised by the capitals in Acronym City. Stopper began to agree when suddenly he stopped, looked over at the commas and then said, 'repetition to close and repetition to open', then he paused thoughtfully again and said 'multiple repetition to limit and limited repetition to multiply. There was a lot about repetition in the unconscious I seem to recall but there were other things too, maybe *u* has a point, or at least a point towards, hmm, psychochemistry, oops I meant psychotherapy, must have been with the Hypothalamus at that point eh? What do you use psychotherapy for, treatment of the clinically depressed?'

'I'd rather say allegedly or apparently depressed' suggested the '**t**'.

'Hmm and when you are depressed, what are the symptoms? Lack of confidence; anxiety, leading to misery... misery...misery, that's it!'

'That's repetition.' Said' '**s**'.

'Surely is, and if it's heading into misery I think I'd rather have the limiting kind of repetition rather than the multiple kind.' '**t**' said.

'No,' said Stopper 'that was repetition to confirm. I do, however, have to visit misery.'

'Hmm, marginally better than misery visiting you I guess,' said Zero.

'Well, hopefully, a lot better my dear, a lot better.'

'Who are you taking with you?'

'Oh, I think my Praetorian guard of commas would be hard to dissuade from accompanying me, but I'd prefer if you three were to stay here and see what you can arrange with the words, whilst I'd like '**u**' and '**s**' to come, and yourself if you'd care to come along Zero?'

This was a smart move by Stopper, he needed to go see misery but he did not really know the intentions of the words, and he really needed to find out what these words really meant and as the commas were extremely adept at slowing words down, and getting between them, and nudging meaning towards some understanding, it made sense to leave this capable trio in charge of things.

Zero agreed to go along so Stopper, an '**s**' and a '**u**', and Zero, all went off in search of misery, leaving the others to approach some words with a view to some verbal exchanges.

It was only a passing word or two but the commas felt their intent was not very supportive of their company, so after quietly warning the others, they headed out to engage in some syntactic persuasion with these suspected malevolent word intentions. The commas positioned themselves just off the page ready to skip in as soon as any untoward sequences began to form, thereby syntactically turning the semantic slope away from their previously intended subject. This was a task at which our three commas were particularly adept as a sequence of well placed commas can severely curtail an intended slight, to, shall we say, a slight intention, then by a punctuational sleight of hand and the application of an e turn the slighter intention off all together. The commas were busy.

In the meantime Stopper and his company found themselves passing words with little direct sense of congruence with their own intention. It wasn't that they didn't know what they themselves were saying, it was that they weren't sure what the words around them were saying, and even less what they meant, but there was a definite feel of less than supportive intention and this feeling grew stronger as they approached the emotional straits. The words were not very keen on the idea of Stopper and co going to meet the emotions as the words themselves felt that they were able to convey any emotions quite adequately thank you very much, and Stopper and co going directly to meet with misery became a bit of a miserable journey to undertake, being surrounded by words that opposed them at every turn. Neither Stopper nor any of the others could know it but it was a bit like walking in a cold slanting rain kind of misery that they felt, so by the time they reached the homes of the emotions and sought out misery, who easily had the biggest home there, they were quite miserable altogether.

Now communication in the emotions was, again, like the communications in the unconscious, more a flow than separate but related groups of words, and, also akin to the unconscious, the communications were non-directional and unavoidable, but, unlike the unconscious, this non-directional, unavoidable, blanket of unreduced perceptions, did in fact have their own inherent syncopated rhythms. Fear was an immersion that had deep long paced pulsing that induced the wish to run like hell. Joy was a light, though still slow, skip of a thing, whereas Misery was a deep, long wave of capture that caught you and kept you discomforted, wary, in an atmosphere of malaise. The emotions didn't leave space as such, as words do, but they weren't constant either, they ebbed and flowed, more akin to a wave than a language, more musical than speech, and so, although music can be open to interpretation, this music left you in no doubt whatsoever as to what you were dealing with. Coming through a strong period of emotion was like being pitched up, spent, and exhausted, on a deserted beach. If there were any words here they were written in the sand.

'My my, but you are one sad group of the unattached if ever I saw one.' Misery said. Misery had a beautiful home and garden, better than any of her neighbours, Joy, Fear, and Lust, and even though there were no chance of Misery ever losing her home to any of the other emotions she was in a constant state of alarm in expectation of losing her home to the other emotions. None of this made any sense but then that's the nature of Misery, very middle class, very repetitive, with a slight turn for the worse. Overall though Misery was actually kind of happy, she just didn't like to admit it.

'Well come in, come in, I've no ink in, don't use it myself, though the words use prodigious amounts in trying to describe me, I'm told.'

'That's a fact.' '*u*' said.

'So, how come you have the biggest home here?' asked Zero.

'Well there's been more misery than any other emotion throughout history Zero, so a little compensation for keeping that going for so long is due.'

'How is keeping the feeling of misery going for so long, beneficial?' asked Stopper.

'The feeling of misery makes you want to improve one's situation by some means or other. Relieve pain, do good things, have good stuff.'

'Why misery? I mean, I can understand the need for pain, fear, and I can definitely appreciate joy, whom I notice has the smallest home here, but why this creeping malaise, misery, Misery?'

'Yes well creeping malaise has it just about right these days in the wealthier parts of the world at least, but if you care to look back through history it's not that long ago that a certain Hobbes chap wrote about the life of man being solitary, nasty, brutish, and short, with the last term seen as a benefit given the other three. The fact is that for the vast majority of the species misery has been their lot for most of existence with only a relatively few having much cause for Joy, which explains the small abode.' Misery replied.

'Yes, but why have the feeling in the first place, would most people not feel better without it?'

'Well yes you could argue that but then where would be the motivation for progress, would the e's have spread their knowledge of good words and sentences had not the lot of most words been fairly mundane at best and positively crap at worst, had the species not been ill treated by the world would they have needed the speed bumps of commas to increase confidence and given time to think? I think not.'

'So the misery is that which can be built on?'

'Yes with luck, work, and endeavour, imagination and a decent supply of necessities, it certainly can.'

'So what's the most common reason for misery?'

'Oh too much bad reality out there and no escape from it, I would think'

'No escape from it? So could repetition, closed repetition, constitute misery for letters and words?'

'Depends on the frequency of repetition, high frequency and short duration becomes attrition over time which would definitely cause misery for any entity with any sense of sentience.'

'Or sentence even?' quipped '*u*'.

'Indeed, what exactly are you after here Stopper?'

'I don't really know, just trying to connect things I do know with what I don't I guess.'

'I still think we'd be a lot better off without you.' cried '*u*'.

'Now '*u*',' Zero said, 'you'll hurt her feelings.'

'Oh '*u*' is just feeling a little out of sorts isn't he?' Misery commented and cast a glance at '*u*', who suddenly felt decidedly queasy.

'Well you lot are used to dealing with words and although the words think they have the emotions covered they haven't really got a handle on us at all, apart from occasional poetry words are more like directions or hints than actual description you might say.'

'Oh yes, like, beyond here there be dragons?'

'Yes, that just about hints in the right direction.'

Yes, but that's not really, a direction.'

'Well there you go again, words are misleading, they indicate resolution, where there is none, they promise information where it is lacking, and they tend to always be slightly disappointing. To really understand the way we emotions work you have to think like you did when you were with the Hypothalamus.'

'Ah yes, of course, but we can't remember what we thought or felt when we were there, that in fact is what we've been trying to do.'

'Well, I would suggest that you've come to the right place for probably the wrong reasons, which is usually the case anyway, words will get you half way there, but you need a leap of faith to cross the gap, what do you think the extended empathetic proximity field is anyway?'

'I thought it was like a semantic field.' Stopper said.

'Yes, it is indeed, but semantics aren't limited to understanding, for a word or sentence to mean something it must feel it. You must feel it.'

Stopper and the others suddenly remembered the feeling of oopsishness they'd felt when they first encountered the Hypothalamus. It was like the sense of that small, virtually nonsensical word oops, was kind of smeared out, spread thin but reaching further than before, as if this extension of its' sense gave it further empathy than it had previously had. Stopper thought about his position in a sentence and realised that in a sense he was beyond words although a good sequence of words would reach beyond him. Stopper could stop words, sentences, and paragraphs, in their tracks but meaning could always slip by like a kind of semantic momentum that just kept going on. Words conveying meaning could be stopped but the content carried on.

Here in the emotions meaning that words would convey was spread out, the semantic field and the emotional state were congruent, though not identical, like two waves, in syncopated motion, rising and falling and rising and falling and rising and falling again.

Misery was a fairly complex emotion and had contact with the Hypothalamus on a frequent basis, whilst Hatred and Disgust were simple instinctive emotions who were informed directly by the Amygdala. Joy, another fairly complex emotion was unhappy that she could not get more work and that when she did she couldn't keep it for long, but then again, that was her nature. Fear was more complex than Hatred and Disgust though not as complex as Joy or Misery, but Fear led more to the latter than the former. Stopper and Zero and the letters with them had collective and personal talks with each of the emotions much of which will be revealed later when they talk amongst themselves and they rejoin the commas and the other letters back in the land of words and relate to them their experiences.

As they left the emotional straits and began their return to words they were a little afraid of what intention the words would have towards them when they returned. Stopper and Zero fell into talking as they travelled back.

'Well Stopper, have you gleaned much from Misery then?'

'Yes, I have, but I'm still cogitating as it were, trying to fit repetition, accumulation and closing in with what she said and how she behaved.'

'Yes, well Misery does seem to be repeated ad nauseam for them so that leads to an accumulation of unhappiness and of course too much misery closes things down, like options and hope.'

'Yes that's a fact, but how is the closing repetition from the unconscious world leaking through to the virtual conscious world, or is it getting in from the real world?'

'How do you mean?'

'Well, back in Acronym City they all but destroyed language as a meaningful form of communication. The capitals and the numbers had twisted it into a means of control and repetition and accumulation were the chief marks of this twist, also much misery was visited on any aspirational letters and even worse on any ill or weakened letters hence the treatment of ghosts.'

Zero shivered at his mention of ghosts, she'd been horrified when Stopper told her about their treatment in Acronym City and she felt an inkling of their fateful fading to nothing akin to the emptiness she sometimes felt in her heart.

'So you're saying that that twisting could happen here?'

'Yes, I'm afraid so, the words are a little afraid of us and already they are forming smaller sentences for protection, they're also simplifying what they are saying, so they can form these sentences quickly so as not to be acronymed. Unfortunately this could set up the very Acronymic Contraction they are trying to avoid. If only I could work out what it is that drives the words to contract so easily maybe then I could get to the source of the problem. They think we are here to setup acronyms ourselves because they are not used to seeing individual letters. I do hope the commas are handling things back there.'

'I have complete faith in the commas as it happens, Stopper, I don't think you need worry about them, and they do have the requisite talents to deal with maladjusted word intentions.'

'True enough', said Stopper, 'True enough.'

The '**s**', '**t**', and '***u***' were also discussing their experiences with the emotions trying to reach some consensus about it between them, they were unsure really about the emotions on their own and they rather felt that a bit of justice wouldn't go amiss for the long term miserable, justice being a word all three of them would be happy to be associated with. The letters didn't realise that the route to justice was through misery, Reason, as a philosopher once said, must be the slave of the passions, that meant that words were meant to convey emotion as best they could, words and sentences could be used to define logic, hard facts with soft words, but when it came to emotions they could only suggest, hint, or signpost. The thing is that the real power of language is in the suggestive, not the hard fact, that Stopper realised at last was what the extended empathetic proximity was about. That's why the capitals hated it so, let language out of their tight control, and you just don't know what those words are going to suggest, I mean, it could lead to disagreement, see, there it goes, the very suggestion!

They arrived back to find the commas finally having a pause in their defence of their little group, so they all retired back to Verbals to catch up with current events. They were just settling in and about to speak when cap C came in and said, 'You have got to see this Stopper, all of you in fact, there's a new development up at the bracket and I think it's the sign of someone from Acronym City you know.'

All of them followed cap C up to the area by the bracket and as they saw the newly constructed building in front of them. It had bright white walls and square windows and a big double door but what really stood out was this bright red roof and that suggested only one character from Acronym City. This was a sign from Red, but what did it mean? Was this a threat or was it good news?

They entered the building where they found some letters placing equal signs down. Suddenly they all realised that they hadn't seen equal signs at all for a very long time where here in front of them were loads of them all in a line. Every so often there were js with their curl round to the outside of the equal sign and the dot was on the outside of the other side. They were all marvelling at this when they heard a whistle in the distance and then came the sound of what sounded like a syncopated wind. What they saw then had never been seen in the virtual world before but coming down the equal signs was a train, but this was no ordinary train. Red had created a ghost train to carry the ghosts through the unconscious quickly enough to get there without any serious harm. As the train came in the ghosts were taken to the ink well centre for, well treatment, though what for, the staff were not to know. Red came to greet Stopper and finally to meet Zero, of whom he was a bit nervous, after all that was some trick she pulled back in the False Front Shop. Mind you Zero was more than a little awe struck herself at the sheer audacity of this Ghost Train: a remarkable feat by any measure.

'Well, Red, welcome, and just how did you manage this then?' asked Stopper.

'You can thank the equal signs and the j's for that, the equal signs were extremely fed up at not being used anymore.' In Acronym City everything was either greater or smaller than everything else. Equality, even as a concept, was made redundant. 'So all of the equal signs got together and came up with this idea of getting together in line. They worked out that this could be useful as a way of holding truth in line as the words were being so damned disappointing in that respect. It was when Red saw this that he had the idea of a running track for some vehicle. Now to run any track vehicle the track must be true and you can't get much truthful than equal signs in line. The j's lended themselves to stability of the line, then they came to me to see about constructing the vehicle which I called a train.'

'Well Red, you've surpassed yourself this time my good red font,' '*u*' said, what's your next project?'

'Next project, not me, '*u*', I'm happy being a ghost train driver, that'll do for me for some time. At least until I've moved all the ghosts in Acronym City.'

'Well that sounds like a permanent job to me, Red, they are always going to produce ghosts in Acronym City, strikes me that that's the nature of the place.'

'A ghost production system, now that's a horror story.'

'Surely is, you know maybe you should bring lower case letters over first, that would stop the ghost production cycle wouldn't it?'

'Sounds like a good idea there, '*u*', but they would just increase the production cycle to compensate, then I'd have to go for ghosts all over again, sometimes you have to help the worst off, because if you save the saveable first you end up creating more unsaveable in the process.'

'Yeah, but what's the use of saving the unsaveable?'

'Well you can't actually save the unsaveable but you can make things better for them, you can give them some semblance of hope, but more important you give the letters on the edge some hope too, and well, hope rises, '*u*', hope rises.'

'Sometimes it does Red, sometimes it does.'

The words had been concerned at the coming of Red, though they were more startled by the ghosts than they were of Red's fine hues. Still, Red's natural, if somewhat piratical, charisma, brought enough words round to make a sentence of things, while Stopper and the commas also brought a few more words through and so, with the help of a colon and a question mark, both of who had long been here, were enough to build a paragraph to hold themselves secure in a fine, lucid, semantic stronghold. Once this was done they set about repeating the process but with other words and soon they had a burgeoning tale as the paragraphs began to link and meaning slipped playfully around in the open streets of this new built literary citadel. Other words and phrases of note would wander through her ample streets, soaking up the atmosphere of rhythm, reason, and much loved side-street raucous rhyme, feeling the warp and the weave of wares waiting to catch your attention and willing, only then, to let you go.

This was a good time for language, for meaning, and for feeling too. The letters were contented in their words and the words were contented in their sentences while both reached out beyond their limited selves and effortlessly stretched to deeper, wider meaning. The ghosts after treatment at the Ink Well were able to get around, though drift was perhaps a more appropriate expression for the way they moved through the paragraphs and tales then told, fleeting, fading, reminders of meanings, once known but now lost, or maybe remembered only dimly now, the ghosts floated by between the lines. Stopper and Red and Zero had met and were kind of drifting through some paragraphs themselves, talking of what they had planned and what had transpired between their previous encounters and how things had turned out. Stopper had neglected to tell Zero the story of the ghosts in Acronym City as he thought she would find it too harrowing a tale even for her, but once Red had arrived with his whistles and his hisses on the ghost train and she had found out about the nature of the passengers, she had cornered Stopper and made him tell the whole story and she had been extremely upset as was Stopper as he related the story, but where Stopper saw what Red had done in bringing ghosts from Acronym City as something fantastic, Zero had far more mixed feelings. She wasn't sure the ghost train was such a great idea and she wasn't sure of Red having never met him in the first place, though had she met him before was no assurance that she would have thought better of him anyway. Stopper understood his nature and what it took to turn around and what it would take to stay in that direction. Red was no conviction letter, he cared for being present more than being good or bad and this nature had given him a presence that could be used for either, so when Red had decided to choose the better path and bring his presence to bear upon it, Stopper felt congratulations were in order.

'I've got to hand it to you Red, I didn't expect to see you again, certainly didn't expect to see you here, but, never in my wildest sentences, could I have anticipated you arriving in a ghost train, that's just about the best reintroduction I could have conceived but I didn't; you did.'

'Whoa, Stopper, you'll have me blushing.'

'Not that anyone would notice Red'

'Hence the rouge, Stopper, my name and nature are both Red to hide my shame.'

'Shame, it's a shame we never met sooner Red, that's all, you dealt with Acronym city the way you had to, now you've dealt with it better, but, enough of this back patting session, how did this ghost train come about Red, there's a tale worth telling here methinks.'

'Ah well, after you and your friends left I had a bit of a think about what you had said, and after thinking awhile decided I had to find ways to distance myself from my previous associates.

'So how did you come to be interested in the ghosts?' Zero asked.

'You can thank Stopper for that, his last big speech in Acronym City gave me a grasp of ghostliness that woke me up and made me realise that we were led by ghosts of their own making, that the capitals had wrapped themselves in numbers to such an extent that it was only the numbers that kept their empty selves as one, and as for the numbers, well they never cared for anyone anyway. I'd never thought of ghosts, in any way or form at all until Stopper gave that speech, and if ghosts can't wake themselves, they can wake others. Stopper, Zero starts more than he stops, and he started me in the right direction.'

'Well, let's hope so', said Zero, who still wasn't completely convinced that the bringing of ghosts from Acronym City was necessarily a good idea, not because she thought the ghosts should not be helped, but because, as Red had said, 'if ghosts can't wake themselves, they can wake others', meaning himself of course, but it was the other others that could be awakened that worried Zero, and she could not help but wonder fearfully of what other other's slumber had been disturbed here. She remained silent on these fears however and simply asked, 'So how did it all come about then?'

'Well I began to ask around quietly about ghosts and at first I have to say there was much denial but then shifty eyes told their own tales, and slowly but surely, the ghost stories emerged in the damp dark environment where they were encamped. There were many tales but little real evidence outside the Humpty Dumpty Factory except, as I was moving around looking for evidence that it seemed didn't exist I began to notice the occasional saucers of ink that were left out. I took little notice at first until I also began to notice that when I returned the saucers were dry. I lay low and got into a position from where I could see two of these saucers and set about making myself comfortable as possible for the long watch. So I lay there watching and after a while felt extremely bored when all of a sudden I saw the level of one of the saucers contents go down in rather too fast a rate for evaporation, unless it was some kind of enhanced evaporation but there was no evidence of any increase in temperature which could result in this. Yet the level went down as I watched and what disappeared from the saucer disappeared from sight. Well I had no idea what was going on here but I saw this happen dozens of times before I saw anything else.'

'What did you see?' asked Zero, who was completely caught up in Red's tale now.

'Well, everything was exactly the same as before when just out of the side of my eye I thought I spied a fleeting tinge of blue, but as soon as I looked it was gone. This happened numerous times and it was only when I told another letter friend of mine that he told me I'd seen a ghost, well half seen more like. Now I knew that they did exist and that they weren't just literary symbols from Stopper, well that got me even more interested than before. So I arranged a visit to the Humpty Dumpty Factory and there I saw it all and Stopper, I understood how you and the commas felt.'

Stopper murmured assent, whilst Zero looked on edge as Red detailed the goings on at the Humpty Dumpty Factory and the way they replaced letters with ghosts and used them and used them and used them and used them and used them and used them again. Sometimes, he told them, the letters become ghosts that replace themselves. Zero shivered at that and Stopper blanched to such a degree that he nearly disappeared against the white backdrop, while Red continued to relate his ghost story, which, as he continued, it began to appear, and feel, as if the words around them were closing in and listening ever closer. Words of course are always aware of other words close by but those words are usually part of the very story they are in, so they were particularly interested in words that were part of a story that they were not in, especially as it referred to the strange half visible letters who had recently arrived. Many words were more than a little troubled by these recent immigrants, though many more could see beyond the half visible and empathise with their plight, but there were the beginnings of strain in some of the sentences not yet detectable but there nonetheless.

Red continued and spoke of bumping into a half seen, half heard, h, literally as it happens, who gave him the information on ghosts from the perspective of the half seen, half heard position. Over time and a good few half conversations with the half silent h, and Red going over these half remembered and half forgotten reminiscences brought forth the full dialogue as it was meant to be in the first place according to Red who being one half of the dialogue was able to fill the gaps as he pleased. Zero looked a little doubtful at this point and Stopper asked if the h was half way to ghostliness to which Red replied that no, that wasn't the case, but that due to the practise of the h often being called on to be silent, he was able to at least half suggest what ghostliness was about and anyway, didn't they know that the h was a consonant? Of course both Zero and Stopper replied we know that, not understanding what Red was getting at, at all. Well, replied Red, then how could h be a ghost? Then suddenly he realised that they didn't know. All the ghosts are vowels he cried and after a brief pause said we have a saying now that only vowels howl. Both Zero and Stopper were stunned at this revelation and they had to digest and try and understand what this meant so they arranged to carry on this discussion with Red at a later time to which Red replied that he would catch them in another paragraph soon. The words around them felt more than a little perturbed at the premature ending of this overheard tale, indeed the vowels in their midst were particularly piqued and even after Red and Zero and Stopper went off, the chatter amongst the words was of ghosts well into the night.

Stopper and Zero had met with the commas, '*u*', '**g**' and '**t**'. They were discussing the fallout of the news that only vowels become ghosts and the question they were asking was whether this was due to the choice of letters by the capitals and numbers or whether the vowels had some inherent property that fated them to be phantoms given the right adverse conditions. Also if the choice was the choice as it were, why did they not ghost consonants?

'Look, vowels are the heart of the language, the heart of every word,' said '*u*', 'you need vowels for speech; they are in fact the breath of language.'

'So, if the capitals want to destroy language they take its breath away?' Zero said

'Strangle it!' Stopper added. 'Yes it's the vowels that give the language breath that make it verbal so the vowels enable the cycle from page to mouth and back, the consonants are the packaging.'

'Which is why they choose the consonants for Acronymic contractions' said Zero

'Not only that.' Said '*u*', 'but if you take out the vowels there is only acronymic contraction left as an option for the consonants.'

''Yes, and if there are no vowels, there are no words for the consonants to package', said '*t*', and then added, 'you get fed up carrying the word lynx around for any length of time I can tell you.'

'How would you know?' asked '*u*'.

'Well, '*l*' is one of my best mates as it happens and it happens quite often.'

'The word lynx, I thought it was fairly rare.'

'No, my friendship with l happens quite often.'

'Then there's the loss of the **e**s contribution.'

'Yes, you know it's almost admirable the way they've thought this through, you wouldn't believe the capitals had it in them.' Stopper said.

'There's nothing admirable about deliberately fading ghosts to oblivion, of making letters enter into Acronymic contraction with no extension, no empathy, and too little proximity, nothing admirable at all.' Zero replied.

'Well I did say it, meaning the action, not the actors, and I did say almost, which is close, but no cigar my dear.'

'It's still too close for comfort, Stopper.'

'Just making the point dear,' Stopper replied somewhat abashed, 'I do agree with you but it is best to know your enemy well you know.'

'I don't have a problem with you knowing your enemy, in fact I can appreciate you respecting your enemy, but admiration is taking things a step too far Stopper, a step too far.'

'Well, Zero, a general can admire the tactics of a general on the other side even though they are in opposition.'

'You are a full stop Stopper, not, a general, and there is a difference, don't get thinking like a capital, speaking of which, just where the hell is cap C, I haven't seen form or font of him in paragraphs.'

'He's taken charge at the station for the ghost train for now, whilst Red recuperates.'

'Celebrate you mean don't you?'

'Yes. Well, that's the way Red is Zero, he's an Acronym City boy, and like they say, you can take the Red out of Acronym City, but you can't take the Acronym City out of Red.'

'Yes, I do understand, but that doesn't mean it doesn't worry me.'

'Will you two stop your semantic sparring and get back to the job in hand?' asked '**g**'.

'Certainly, my lower case letter friend,' replied Zero, 'but until you realise that semantic sparring is the job in hand, the capitals are going to put you in an Acronym for your lack of understanding, not for punishment mind, or even recuperation come to think of it, but for celebration of the dumbness of the unattached letter.'

'Ouch, steady on Zero, we were all feeling a tad unattached at your apparent private semantic sparring, that's all I really meant.'

'Yes, Zero, steady on, anyway they were doing a bit of semantic sparring of their own back there with the lynx I do recall.'

Zero gave Stopper one of her withering blank stares and everyone fell quiet, then the commas arrived and the tone changed completely, the build up of paragraphs continued apace, their conversation turned lighter as they felt recent pressures lift from them. Overall they began to feel that things were much better now, they were safe and secure in the spaces between the words and they walked between sentences at their leisure. Red had rescued the ghosts and really speaking, even Stopper started to feel that maybe they were all right. The state of language was healthy and robust as disparate topics crossed one another, danced with each other, and then went off with some other, sentences twisted and turned and wriggled and giggled their way round their subjects and all of the hubbub, bubble, and trouble was far from their minds.

'How's thing's going over there?' called '**g**' from one paragraph to another, whereby '**t**' answered, 'Absolutely fine, words are just falling into place, meanings sprouting all over the place, tales are growing of daring deeds and long felt needs.'

Other calls were passing to and fro between paragraphs all confirming the growing of a story waiting to be told of a time when letters got along with one another, when punctuation marks and letters respected each other, and when stories sidetracked with no fear of losing overall sight of the trail. Making their way between some words Zero,

Red, and Stopper were hearing the rest of Red's ghost stories and also preparing to wish him well on another trip on the ghost train. Red told them how although the saving of ghosts was apparently impossible, it struck Red that even so, it could not but be a good thing to at least try, after all there had never been this many ghosts in one place at one time before, and maybe the accumulation of ghosts would have a different effect on the ultimate outcome. So, despite the fact that the rescuing of ghosts would inevitably send some more letters into wraith-like swoons of anticipatory anxiety regarding both their current and upcoming condition to be page worthy, Red decided that, be that as it may, help for the helpless was a steeper semantic slope to climb and therefore worth it, the hosts of letters slow and shallow slide notwithstanding, as this high calling would be more worthy of note and thereby more likely to save a few letters by generating a headline and an article of note to follow. As said before, you could take Red out of Acronym City, but you could not extract Acronym City from Red. Stopper, who was used to Reds somewhat perverse logic kind of understood that whilst the surrounding reasons for his decision were bound to be more than a little suspect, the central decision had been taken in good heart. Zero, a little more circumspect as to Reds moral universe said not a thing. Red, oblivious to the finer points of things bid a hearty farewell to his new-found friends and set off for the station and the next run on the ghost train.

So off went Red as the commas came along and the five of them went along to Syntax to listen to some of the rhythm groups there and proceeded to argue whether rhythm came before meaning or did meaning give rise to rhythm. The commas reckoned that rhythm came after meaning to give it some pizzazz, but Stopper thought that rhythm gave rise to meaning by making connections never heard before and it happens, he said, that syntactic and semantics are both about making connections, twisting them, turning them, and making them anew. As Red was about to enter the station he paused and looked out over the tale he was just about to leave. There sweeping below him were sentences and paragraphs, wide semantic boulevards, chapters and interludes as far as the eye could see. Red was pleased he had come here, glad he had built the ghost train, and ecstatically happy to be driving it, so he turned and he entered the station then he boarded the train and off he went with a whistle and a bang. The train pulled out of the station, semantic carriages pulling over syntactical rails in a narrative drive to rescue some ghosts.

Everything was peaceful in the land of words and sentences until the ghost train came in. No-one paid any attention to it at first but it was what wasn't there that caught the nearby words and letters attention. There were no ghosts and there was no Red. Indeed for a long time no-one left the train until a capital G and a number 3 came off to have some furtive looks around. After briefly scouting around they turned and beckoned the rest of the unseen passengers from the shadow of the station. A host of capitals and numbers came first followed by another host of lower case letters amongst whom there was a fearful excitement betrayed by a fervent energy that could not be contained.

Way back in the middle of the paragraphs Stopper, Zero, and the commas, '*u*', '*t*', and '*g*' were blissfully unaware of any difference in the story they were in until the chant, only half heard at first, but as the short sharp end of 'it' became audible, Stopper grew immediately tense and '*u*' looked increasingly nervous as the full sound was now heard, again and again and again: Stop it! Stop it!

Stop it! The Stop-its had arrived. Stopper sent word to the words to retrieve some words of intelligence to try and find out what they were here for, though you would have to be dumb as a doorknob not to guess that from the only word they seemed to know, but he needed to find out how they hoped to proceed in their ceaseless attempt to cease, when there was this wonderful story to join in should they choose to. Stopper as an expert in hindsight and furthermore a well experienced champion of the completion of tales was confident that persuasion of the advantages of being a part of a tale well told would be impossible to ignore. Stopper however was unaware of just how indoctrinated in the vertical way these letters were and more important had no conception of just how ridiculously stupid they were. None of them had given a thought as to Red or the ghosts at that point as they had no idea that they were missing in the first place. When they did hear of the missing ghosts and Red, Stopper wanted to send out a search party and was in fact just setting this up when word came back that any search party would have to be cancelled as the stop its had begun their attack and there was now no way through to the station.

Any news of Red and his ghostly company would have to wait for either Red himself to reappear and deliver such news himself which was a situation to be hoped for, or, the ghosts would have to get through the unconscious which Stopper had no hope for at all. There was no way that these ghosts, once off of the train could survive the onslaught of the unconscious where there was no extended empathetic proximity, field or otherwise, not that they would be able to access it anyway, even if it were there. Ghosts couldn't do that. Ghosts, however, were lingerers if ever there were, and having lingered in Acronym City for some time with no real support save the occasional saucer of ink, lingering in the unconscious didn't seem that much more of a hardship. Ghosts getting out of the unconscious though, now that was more than a little unlikely, and none were expected to be seen again this side of Acronym City.

This side of Acronym City though was becoming a place of some turmoil as the Stop-its began their assault on the paragraphs nearest the station. As kind of befit the single issue Stop-its, they mounted their attacks by assaulting single words. The capitals had done some research, if you could call it that, and had found where words had appeared in other sentences where either the connotation or the immediate environment was of a somewhat questionable status, or at least it would be if you ignored completely what language is supposed to do, which they of course did. This research by the way had been carried out in the libraries that the capitals were now busy closing down and there was nothing ironic about that, nothing at all. They then directed the Stop-its to attack the word in question. This they did in a kind of sneering repetition that backed up the accusations coming from the capitals. The words around the accused word stuck up for their sentence companions arguing that of course the word had been in a different sentence before and that it had had a different meaning from now. That, after all, was what language was for! As for the word being involved in a questionable utterance, well, there were the connotations to take into account, then there were the circumstances of the character, the possible oppositional character, and so on but all to no avail. Indeed, after a while, the Stop-its didn't even bother with accusations at all, just repetition, and sneering, it seems, sufficed. The arguments made no sense at all but that did not stop them repeating them forever and a day. So, even though the word under attack was completely innocent this constant sneering did have its effect in time; first the surrounding words would get a little uneasy, which would of course affect the accused word; until in time the offending word felt too self conscious to stay in the sentence. Meaning had to mould itself to this new reality without losing too much of its direction. It was obvious that this technique of repetition and attrition was beginning to have a disastrous effect on the story, and was even bringing the not yet written end into some doubt! Stopper was mortified.

Another Form of attack was on any kind of ambiguity in a sentence as a covert method of hiding the truth. Now, that was kind of ironic when you think about the Humpty Dumpty factory. The argument of course is nonsense but by now the sentences were getting nervous never knowing who was about to be attacked next, not to mention the now constant rearrangement necessary to just try and hold to some meaning not too distant from what it was before. In order to avoid the ambiguity attacks some of the sentences began to take action themselves by shortening themselves and simplifying what they said. As the sentences did this it led to further turmoil throughout the paragraph, but the words were nervous. The trouble was that where the longer sentences, being by and large of more intelligence, could see that shortening sentences to avoid potential shortening of the same sentence didn't make any sense, for a sentence anyway, but the shorter sentences who were a bit dumb anyway, shortened themselves and got dumber still. The real irony of course is that the self shortening sentences were doing the Stop-its jobs for them, but then again the real, real irony is that the Stop-its were making the very thing that they wanted to stop worse and thereby harder by far to stop. Mind you if you want to talk about dumb, the Stop-its are the champions of dumb. The capitals of course were very pleased with their work.

Stopper, deeper into the story was trying to set up defences, and to do so he called on the commas, who were particularly adept at this kind of sentence defence. He instructed them to keep changing the meaning of sentences by creative placement of themselves coupled with logophilic perambulation in order to keep any changed meaning away from the overall meaning of the paragraph. Stopper further suggested to all of the paragraphs that they practise this logophilic perambulation using their own commas, colons and semi-colons, as a means of not settling on any vulnerable meanings whilst under attack, thereby giving the attackers no point of entry to carry out their semantic destruction.

The area around the station was completely lost now, so the defence was concentrated in the next part of the story, and it took a long time before the capitals, full of sound and fury, realised that the tale was no longer told by an idiot, that this tale signified more than nothing, that the destruction of this entire story was no longer a foregone conclusion, for it was not yet written and the capitals were particularly poor writers, never considering any meaning past themselves. Still, they could attack and destroy all of the story up to the unwritten part so it would at least look like a tale told by an idiot, but the commas were being a damned nuisance, the colons were bloody revolting, and the semi-colons were an absolute disgrace! What was an enterprising capital to do these days?

The suggestion that they get back to Acronym City and take the Stop-its with them uttered by a few busy punctuation marks were largely ignored by all accounts. The battle for meaning in what became known as the Great Semantic Stand Off was in flux at the moment, this being the name given to the more dynamically punctuated paragraphs near the front, and while you couldn't really say that the defence was gaining the upper hand, seeing as how that wouldn't really be defence as such, you could definitely say that the capital tide had been repulsed and the Stop-its were growing hoarse. The paragraphs were rearranging themselves and slow but sure the original meaning was beginning to reassert itself and earlier intentions regained their earlier intentions.

As the story began at last to settle on the page, the capitals consulted with the numbers to try and work out a strategy to swing the battle their way again. The numbers were, as always, largely unconcerned, and they quietly sent word to bring the comma detail forward. A few moments later the de-tailed commas from loads and loads of paragraphs ago were forcibly marched, though that couldn't be described as the most accurate word for their particular form of locomotion, in. The numbers explained that these detailed commas were essentially stuck between being commas and full stops, but they were neither of the two. They had previously been commas but they were now not quite full, full stops, and if you wanted to battle an unfulfilled full stop then a few not quite full full stops were very handy. What, the numbers asked the capitals, do you get between commas and full stops? The capitals had no answer to that. You get the semantic focus of the sentence, the numbers told them, now do you get the meaning of that? They, predictably, didn't. Ah, a one, a two, a one – two – three: unleash the not quite fulls!

The paragraphs at the front never knew what hit them and it took some time before the commas and the other 'cause to pause' punctuation marks realised that the sentences were getting very confused and this was no time for wavering sentences. Paragraphs began to crumble, and then the always wordless, often speechless, letters were taken, shaken and confused, to join the Stop-it gang and forced to join in the single issue chants on pain of a short ride on the ghost train and the promise of wordlessness for the entire story, which was a bit much all things considered.

Our three commas: Alecto; Tisiphone; and Megaera; were in serious danger of realising their full Erinyes projections, when Alecto heard her name being repeatedly called in the middle of a sentence. Investigating she came upon one of the de-tailed commas who quickly explained what was going on and how she had ended up in this situation and how sorry she was for the confusion that inevitably ensued. Alecto quietened her by reminding her that it was better than being deep fried, an avoided alternative the de-tailed comma could not possibly disagree with, although she did mention that should this story completely fail then Acronym city and the deep fried fate may fall to them all. The sentences had been confused by accepting the de-tailed commas as commas then thinking of them as full stops. The de-tailed commas told Alecto that they were only trying to do what the other commas were doing, that they were driven to do that and had no choice, but that their post comma fate distorted their every venture and they were well fed up having been in this state since way back in the first part of the story, and you can't really blame us for that now, can you, they said. Alecto asked how many of them there were and then went off to find the other two commas to prevent the Erinyes from exploding onto the scene prematurely.

They decided that they would have to sacrifice a few paragraphs, but they would try and quietly recycle the lost words and letters back into their replacements. Now that they knew that some of the lost letters were being forced into Stop-it gangs they felt that if they could make contact with them then they could set up this recycling paragraphs tactic as a way of hopefully allowing the capitals to think they were winning whilst quietly enabling their eventual defeat. This was a good plan, and it did work for some time, unfortunately this plan was overheard by some words in the story and at least one of them later related this to the capitals in the hope that they would get a better position amongst the Stop-its, whom they had long had great sympathy for they insisted, which just goes to show that you can't believe a word sometimes.

It turned out that the word involved was one of those words that was particularly nervous, if that's the right word, of the coming of the ghosts, and rather felt that they had brought the neighbourhood of the paragraph down in a somewhat indistinct way of telling. So when the word heard that the ghosts had been thrown off of the train which meant their non-arrival in their neighbourhood they could not help but feel good about that aspect of it. A rather circumspect way of putting it, it must be said. Suffice to say, that although this word was not itself racist or anti-immigration, the word was somewhat closer to the latter than it was to empathy, of that there was no doubt whatsoever. Still it does take all sorts to make up a sentence and even more sorts to make up a paragraph even if the Stop-its they were about to join were not of that opinion, for if they were, that would render their particular type of attacks somewhat disingenuous would it not?

Anyway after this unfortunate episode Alecto and the others found it more and more difficult to recycle the paragraphs as they found less and less of letters of note available. So once again they began to lose paragraphs to the capitals and the battle was going against them. They were having a particularly bad time of it when suddenly the chant of the stop-its changed both wording and focus which brought instant relief to a good many stressed out sentences. The new wording was in fact, 'dirty pinko', which was directed at what looked like a dirty pink letter that may or may not have been an r, but it was difficult to tell as it was so worn, tattered, and torn. Stopper immediately gleaned that it was Red looking much the worse for wear and needing urgent treatment at the Ink Well. Unfortunately the Ink Well was now under the command of the capitals and they and the stop-its even more, looked on Red as a traitor, a turncoat, and a dirty pinko to boot. So Red was turned away from the Ink Well in a most unseemly fashion. Sad to say, many of the letters and words in the defending paragraphs had rather mixed feelings about him such that though they were loath to see him treated that way and they were glad that he had gotten back, they still held him much to blame for the mess they were now in for without the ghost train this would never have happened. Red, or dirty pinko, was simply left but then suddenly the sneering stop-its quailed as a host of ghosts rushed through their ranks and up to find a bedraggled Red whom they gently lifted and bore him away far beyond the paragraphs currently in turmoil.

Red was explaining what had happened when the Stop-its and the capitals had taken over the ghost train. Red still looked a bit of a pinko and more than a little bedraggled but he was no longer a dirty pinko, except no doubt to any Stop-its, but there were none of them in this vicinity. Stopper remarked that it was a bit of a shame they didn't have a False Font Front Shop here if only to help Red feel better until he felt better. Red replied that actually he did feel considerably much better than he looked and that it was probably best that he looked a bit off colour as it were, because that saved him from going back a few paragraphs and joining the fray.

'So what happened, how did they take over the train Red?' Stopper asked.

'Well, the last two trips we carried some lower case letters over as well as ghosts and it was looking like more of the same again as we pulled out of Acronym City. Now, we were allowing anyone who wanted on the train by this time, reasoning that anyone who wanted out of Acronym City were fine by me, so it never crossed my mind that the Stop-its would not only get on the train but actually take it over, I mean, I expected some cat calls and more than a few murmurs and the like for my turning against them but I had no idea of how despicably they would treat the ghosts, I mean I still feel angry about that when I think of it.' Red fell silent for a while as he pulled himself together again.

The commas remembered the way the letters and numbers at the Humpty Dumpty Factory treated the ghosts and were not really surprised, and Zero said that it was probably a kind of displaced contempt for their own vulnerability to fading to phantoms themselves that explained it, but that did not, she added, justify it at all.

After describing as best he could the appalling treatment handed to the ghosts and the completely uncaring attitude to their fate shown by the Stop-its, Red still could not understand how they could treat ghosts who hadn't done the Stop-its any harm, or anyone else for that manner, could be worse treated than one who had turned against them after leading them for so long, namely Red himself. Red felt guilty about this, even though it was not his fault. However we shall pass over this mistreatment of the ghosts, there being nothing really new in such a report other than a tired reminder of normality in Acronym City. Red of course was not left alone but was severely beaten and battered to such an extent that he could barely rise from the page for some time. When he came to as it were he was surrounded by all the ghosts waiting quietly around him. Now this was a shock to our piratical speaker, as ghosts were expected to fade away almost instantly to nothing in the unconscious but here they were quietly waiting to talk, with no wailing, and no quailing, and no fear.

The ghosts told Red that they'd found a story lingering in the unconscious, and that it had passed this way before but that it was so strong that it had remained, like a trail of a tale, and that the ghosts, all vowels, could take their place in the trail of words and be complete again, and there they would be content and that they thought there were enough words and enough ghosts to lead Red through the story and out the other side. Red then protested that he could surely make it through himself but the ghost nearest him told him wryly that he was almost as opaque as the rest of them. It was the only time anyone had ever heard humour from a ghost said Red, and it had to be an opaque one: a truly translucent moment if ever there was.

'For it is written.' Red finished with a wide piratical grin which definitely brightened his look up for the first time in a while. Indeed, Red, not having been in the tale much of late and perhaps more so when he had, had had little to grin about for some time anyway. Still it seemed that piratical grins were definitely the flavour of this particular paragraph, as Red would have said, had he not been piratically grinning so wide that he couldn't actually speak at that point. The story they'd found was the story of your journey through there Stopper. Your story saved the ghosts, who saved me...Red fell silent, and his phantom attendants indicated that he needed to rest. As they were leaving, *u* asked if the train was still usable, to which Red replied that, yes the train as long as you can run a train off the rails, which he further explained by saying that after the train was taken over all of the *j*s got off of the rails and all of the equals signs came here, but the *i*s who had been on the train had all gone to Acronym City and that, ended Red, was an unparalleled event.

'How did the ghosts find the story and how did they get into it, I don't really understand that?' asked '*u*'.

I think,' said Zero, 'that in the unconscious there is no extended empathic proximity field but there is a chemical field and that communication in there is done by a combination of chemical and electrical fields, so the ghosts it seems were able to arrange the remains of their chemical nature by using the electrical and chemical fields as guides and thereby become part of the story, and it seems that this was helped a great deal by the fact that the Hypothalamus was so enamoured of his particular part in this tale that he has, by all accounts, been retelling it repeatedly.'

'That is such a nice ending for those ghosts; it really is,' Stopper said quietly as they made their way back towards the centre of the story, 'really neat..., in fact, really, really, neat.'

Zero looked towards Stopper with some wry but hopeful looks as she perceived what was likely shaping in his dark head.

Stopper and Zero were now in Buzzwords, a short stop cafe supplying instant, if somewhat shallow semantic refreshment, but they needed to stop a while and reassess the entire situation in the light of all of the new information, so a place with minimum semantic interference was ideal under the circumstances.

The news of the **i**s going off to Acronym city was still to be digested, along with the somewhat more easily digestible fact of the equal signs coming back here being inevitable given the fact that they were needed to bring the train home, plus, of course, equal signs aren't very welcome in Acronym City, but then again why would the *i*s want to be there?

'After all,' Stopper remarked, 'wouldn't they just be ghosted as soon as they got there?'

'No,' said Zero, 'the '**i**' is the one vowel that they don't ghost.'

'They don't,' Stopper said, 'I didn't know that, why not?'

'Well, it seems that the capitals don't see the '**i**' as the breath of the language, them being a kind of clipped vowel sound most of the time, they're not open like the other vowels so the capitals don't use them.'

'You mean they don't use them for that.'

'Yes, I guess I do.'

'Hmm so what do they use them for?'

'That's something Red never told us.'

'Maybe he doesn't know?'

'Possible, mind, he was always more interested in his own position and status in reference to any others rather than the other way around and the colour red does tend to stand out in the middle of a sentence, so he may not know, but could be worth asking next time we meet though.'

'Yes, I'm more concerned about the curtailed commas, to tell the truth. I mean apart from the obvious effectiveness of their use, it's the fact that it demonstrates that this whole attack was planned for some considerable time.'

'Yes this has been gestating for a very long time, so how many more surprises do they have?'

'I don't know but I may just have some surprises of my own yet.'

'What are you thinking Stopper?'

'Oh, best that stays unsaid for now, Zero dear, even to you; even to you.'

As they left buzzwords and wound their way between the lines in the quiet of the passages they could hear the almost ever present chant of 'stop it, stop it, stop it', in the distance, and Stopper knew that one way or another, or even another still, he would have to find a way to stop it, but what wanted stopping; and what wanted starting; and what, in the end would have to continue on; what would he end up looking back on; what would the fate he saw stretching behind them be: for full stops in the end, are like a too tired Tiresias; tired of every other's futures, and ever looking back, seeing never satiated Fate in her grotesque threads of finery, weaving her witless way to the present, spinning her wasted webs to stick down the past lest it rise and ignore her heartless hospitality. Tiresias knew that hospitality well. Stopper knew that he had to weave enough threads to link the past to the future, to thread some way through the eye of the needle of time, to push back Fate a while longer. It was Stoppers job to defer to the needs of the moment and those needs were to protect the story in place, and if in doing that he could gainsay Fate, for a while at least, well, that would be worth doing; he had never been keen on characters that wanted too much and Fate was Avarice Incarnate.

Avarice Incarnate of course, was not to be toyed with, hard to avoid, and impossible to get round, but, thought Stopper, greedy little monsters could be defeated, so Stopper went off in search of the commas, whom he found in the company of the slippery letter 's', who Stopper was also gratified to find, for commas alone were no match for Fate. The Furies though, were born of the injustice of Fate in the first place, whilst the Graces themselves had been a celebration of all that was best prior to the injudicious interventions of Fate, so the commas had good reason to be involved in any attempt to circumvent the vast outreaching grasp of Fate. Fate's greatest attributes were her certainty and her avarice and the very certainty of that avarice could, Stopper told s and the commas, be her weakness too. So, Operation Tempting Fate was conceived. The term itself came from the commas who had indicated that they were tempting fate by leaving the fray to be here as the stop-its were making ground against them in the early paragraphs. They explained that as well as the attacks on single words and phrases they had also bought in some new attacks that used short and repetitive slurs on various words, phrases, and their associations, and though these attacks were seemingly less direct, they were in fact more effective and the associative effects were multiplying their successes. They had actually been to see 's' to ask if his particular talents in the plurality stakes could be of any use to them in the Great Battle of the Paragraphs. As it happened 's' couldn't see any way he could be of help in the paragraphs but Stopper could now see that s's peculiar plurality talents could be of some use in taking on Fate.

Initially the commas were not keen on this attempt to beat Fate, and did in fact accuse Stopper of being a Captain Ahab after the great white whale. Stopper replied that

where Ahab was the chaser he was not, for like everyone
else he was being chased by Fate, who was always behind
you, slowly inexorably catching you up to lock and stick you
down. Something, said 's', that can't be avoided can't be
beaten. Maybe not, said Stopper but she can be accepted
on better terms than she allows, if you can loop a narrative
around her that is, which is where you four come in. Stopper
explained his idea of how to beat Fate, and as he elucidated
his thoughts one comma, two commas, the 's', and finally
the third comma, came to believe that it actually could be
achieved. They were still worried that taking on this fight
would lose them the other fight, but Stopper assured them
that come their encounter with Fate, there would be no
fighting in the paragraphs whatsoever. He also said that
once they had dealt with Fate, Red would return and the
Battle of the Paragraphs could be resumed and hopefully
won. The loss of Fate will be a fatal blow to the Stop-its,
and though the capitals and the numbers couldn't care less
whether Fate is there or not, the Stop-its will lose heart
and neither the capitals nor the numbers will care to face
the Furies newly victorious over Fate. They asked Stopper
what he was up to but Stopper just smiled and quietly left
the sentence. As for the commas and the 's', they called on
some spare letters and busied themselves constructing a fine
static sentence a little way out of the main story for them to
reside in and there they quietly awaited their Fate.

A few paragraphs from the battle zone, 't' and '*u*' were
talking about **i**'s dismal performance in the battle where,
like the commas and colons and semi-colons they were
supposed to move in to sentences near the battle lines and
unobtrusively blend in to carefully chosen words to alter
their meaning without being noticed, but '**i**' had been
behaving more like his preening capital than a lower case

'**i**', and had been imposing his self on the letters next to him thereby making the change noticeable which was not the way for this to be done at all. Lower cases are not supposed to behave like capitals they were saying and they couldn't understand it at all. They had decided that it would be best to tell Zero and get '**i**' pulled out of the battle paragraphs and have him do something else. They were just about to go off to find Zero when '**t**' spotted a ripple in the Stop-its ranks behind the lines and pointed it out to '**u**'. What, asked '**t**', do you make of that?

The Stop-its at the front were shouting their usual selection of insults, attacking individual letters for past word employment, words for telling lies, phrases for telling too much and so on, and they were using their panoply of short sharp phrases, of single word attacks and letter mispronounces to keep the attack going. Behind them the Stop-its repeated everything the front rank said but just a syllable or two behind. Behind them the Stop-its in the rearward ranks were chanting Stop-it with their usual vigour, but *t* had noticed that that very vigour was fading and coming back as if a ripple of quiet was stealing along their lines. They now noticed that not only was the ripple continuing its path but it seemed to be deepening and broadening, but neither '**u**' nor '**t**' could hazard a guess as to what was causing the ripple. Suddenly they spotted a line of capitals making their way into the ranks of the Stop-its and they were heading in the direction of this sonic ripple. As the capitals made their way they also caused their own sonic ripple as the two slowly and quietly neared each other then the two ripples appeared to combine and spread out into an oasis of calm as the stop-its all fell silent. This of course gave the defending paragraph a chance to regroup and mount a new set of semantic defences but neither t nor '*u*' had any inkling of what was going on and as things were looking a bit calmer they decided to seek out Zero and communicate their concerns regarding '**i**'.

Stopper was moving quietly between the lines of the Stop-its being careful only to be noticeable as he actually passed, thereby ensuring that the Stop-its would all turn in his direction and not towards each other, so avoiding Stop-it communication setting off any alarms. In addition the effect of his motion between the ranks had the marvellously beneficial effect of quieting down the chanting, and it also set up a whisper of '*Stopper*' which it had to be admitted was quite pleasant to the ear as well as muffling the chants in the ranks. A secondary effect was set up at the same time whereby due to the noticeable lack of commotion there, a quiet rumour was set in motion pertaining to the likely cause of this peaceful interlude, the direction of this rumour being, of course, in the opposite direction to Stoppers travels. From beyond the ranks the capitals had noticed the ripple of quietude snaking its way through the ranks and three of them set off to investigate, whereby the Stop-its in the line increased the decibel level of their protests, this was however preceded by a bow wave of rumour that betrayed the presence of the capitals prior to their appearance, which allowed Stopper to nip between a line of stop-its and continue his quiet travels unseen by the capitals who having travelling into the oasis of silence elected to follow the generally louder path of the rumour rather than the quieter path that to the capitals was deemed less likely to be of any consequence.

The net result that whilst the capitals were getting more and more frustrated in their efforts to find the source of quiet, and fervently wishing for a noisy adversary being much easier to find, Stopper was quietly creating a nest bed of Stopper whisperers which was deducting from the Stop-its, but even better, the capitals were stopping the Stop-it's too as they asked them to hush so they could hear the quiet better hoping to find their prey.

Across in the defending paragraphs, letters and punctuation marks and words were rearranging their order and meaning within the constraints of the story, so as to confuse the attackers with greater ease. So, all in all, the story felt a little better about itself, to be honest, what with all this chopping and changing orders and meanings and working within the constraints of the overall tale, had given the tale itself a better understanding of what it actually meant, and that made it a happy tale indeed, at least as happy as it could be under the circumstances.

In the meantime the pluralisation specialist and our commas, graces, and furies, were awaiting Fate, with '**s**' busy pluralising threads and spreading them wide in operation Tempting Fate. Now, with everything ready, they settled down with more than a little trepidation, which suddenly increased enormously as Fate approached with what they hoped were ever widening avaricious eyes. Now '**s**' had been careful to lay the threads towards different sentences which he was sure she would also covet, the sentences involved weren't too happy at the time, but s assured them that Fate wouldn't touch them. So three commas, three threads, and three sentences, all going in different directions, awaiting Fates fateful decision. Fate, eying the three prizes with increasing desire, wished to waste no time for Stopper was who she was really stalking, but one can't leave such presents unaccepted thought she, so in order to grab the merchandise and run, Fate split into three and became the Fates: Clotho; the spinner, with her sticky webs; Lachesis; the allotter, she who gave you what you had, not known for her generosity as it happens, and finally; Atropos, the inexorable, and each of them went for their apportioned thread. Atropos approached Alecto, the unceasing, whilst Lachesis approached Magaera, the grudging one, and Clotho approached Tisiphone, the avenger, though the Fates did not at that point know them to be there. As the Fates began to stick the multiple threads that '**s**' had cleverly prepared, (amazing what a little creative repetition can do) the commas hopped out and skipped behind them before transforming themselves into the full grandiosity of the Furies and as the Furies and the Fates faced up to each other the sentences nearby became increasingly italicised.

So there they were, the spinner facing the avenger, the grudger the allotter, and the inexorable the unceasing, the battle about to be joined, when Lachesis shrieked out, 'Is that you Magaera? Can it really be you?'

'Lachesis! I don't bloody believe it, it must be, what, three millennia since we met! How the hell are you?'

Clotho then hugged Tisiphone, and Atropos and Alecto broke into mutual grins of mucho mutual appreciation.

'Well, it's a long fall from Fury to Grace but it's a lot longer to the call of punctuation, Alecto, how'd you three get into this game then?'

'As a fate you needn't pretend that you don't know.' Alecto replied to Tisiphone who had asked the question.

'Sure we do, but knowing everything that's been may well have some good points ladies, but memory is apt to suffer, so jog our memories dears would you, we're in no rush to go back into her and we promise to let you win this one, as it were, Alecto my sweet, if you would relate the much recorded, yet more forgotten, tale for our fitful, fateful delight, let us rest and tell our tales, here between the lines for some time, we have three millennia to catch up on and a rest is always a good thing, so is there anywhere we could go so as to ease the pressure on these poor strained sentences?'

Magaera, consulted with her partners, and they decided that they should retire from the sentences and make their way to Margins, allegedly a good place to compare notes, and what, with half a millennia each to play with, notes would be a handy reference tool to have nearby. As they settled in the Margins, they renewed their banter.

'Well we certainly remember you three, my, my, you were angry, spitting, quite beguiling at the time as I recall, and so, so, so, responsible too.' Lachesis murmured softly and fondly.

'Well, there wasn't much justice back then was there?'

'No, but you think that's improved? It never improves, Alecto, there is always need for angry ones...

'Oh yes, and were you angry,' Clotho added with a laugh, 'you were the first we ever feared you know.'

'You don't know that much when you're that angry.' Magaera said.

'No, I guess not, but you knew enough to be angry, and many have forgotten even that now.' said Atropos.

So they settled down and exchanged stories of three millennia, the Fates telling of their victories and of their own downfall when the three became one, whilst the Furies told how as the penchant for Angry women faded after the first millennia or so, and how then they elected to becoming the kindly ones, softening their image, then the final transformation to the Graces where they took the names, Aglea, Euphroesine, and Thalia, in an era when Beauty was held to be of the highest in esteem. The Fates listened in rapt attention to this becalming nature of time, but what they were most interested in was how they had ever gotten into the language game, how had they gone from grace to pacing sentences?

'Well, I must admit,' said Magaera, 'we never thought that it would go that way ourselves...but the way things took off, after that printing press, you know that's what really kicked off the Reformation and the Enlightenment! It was the spread of knowledge that fed into both those movements, simple as that, communication made both those movements work, and it was the combination of those movements that have brought us all of the worthwhile things we have, so, literature became all the rage, if you'll pardon the language, and much though we enjoyed our time as the Graces, we felt that the Graces only held responsibility for themselves, we needed to get into language and we needed something worthwhile, responsible, and right, so commas we became, and proud of it too.'

'Yes we are,' added Tisiphone, 'and that was when the es began their great spread and then we had a hand in slowing speech down and imparting confidence. Literature has been our preference for a long time now, we can channel fury and beauty in here, humour, pathos,' to which Alecto added, 'and even take the piss.'

'So now your beloved tales are under threat?'

'Yes they are, even if they are tales that only take the piss, but what of your tale sisters, a tragedy to be recorded in highest literary language unless I am mistaken.'

The commas were particularly interested in how the Fates had become Fate, of how Lachesis, Atropos, and Chlotho, became Moira, known as Fate, and as the Fates told their tragic tale, none of them noticed the hush that had gathered round the story, and the commas, enraptured in the tale of the Fates, were blissfully unaware of the gathering whisper of '*Stopper*' that was susurrating through the sentences beyond the margins.

The whispering wisped away, and what could only be described as an italicised silence ensued. Murmurs followed, grumbles came, and mumbles faded into words unspoken, then the silence rushed its ending in a communal breath from the Stop-its: 'Stopper!' The Capitals took Stopper away.

Farther in to the Tale words were moving shiftily in the ranks of the paragraphs, letters looked to left and then to right, Zero, knew that something strange was happening but she didn't know what, whilst '*u*' and '*t*' and '*i*' were still unaware of what had transpired. The Furies and the Fates were lost in the tales of Oblivion and none knew what should be done until Red came down by the sentences once more and when he got to the battle front the cries from the Stop-its, 'Dirty pinko.' broke upon the silence of the tale as then told.

As the chant 'Dirty Pinko' grew in volume the Furies and the Fates had now parted, and the Furies journeyed down to join Red. They followed the sentences that spoke of the defeat of the Fates by the Furies, and although this was not strictly true, it was permitted, as the truth would be revealed in the passages yet to come. The Furies back in their more comely form of the commas joined Red and were then informed that the Stop-its had Stopper. Oh well, they replied, looks like another change of garb then, and they told Red of the fateful sentences then passing. Red in his dirty pink appearance was no longer the fearsome font he once was and the Stop-its chanted away with derision, taunting his fall from the full font of old, Red stepped forward and stood there stock still for some time, then with one sure smooth move he cast off his dirty pink false font front and stood there shining with a burnished burgundy glow, and the chant from the Stop-its grew faint and lost heart.

Just then the news of the Fates reached the Stop-its and they quailed and they wailed at their now perceived fate. The Furies advanced on the Stop-its who tried vainly to press themselves into the paper to no avail, and the Furies contented themselves with less than fierce admonishments, morphing through Grace to commas as they appeared less than fit for any kind of fight. Plain speech was called for here, for any hint of ambiguity would inevitably, indubitably even, upset them. At which point the commas were arguing whether it was better to pause just there, or wait a little and pause just there, ah yes, said Alecto, but if we were to pause here, the meaning would be shifted. Ah, but the Stop-its were a tad unimpressed by the wonders of word arrangement at that time.

The capitals and the numbers sent for Stopper whom they had placed in the same cage as the detailed commas so when the lower case letter appointed to bring him, the letter had no way of telling who was who. So when he opened the cage he asked which one was Stopper. Stopper, about to reply, was stopped as one of the detailed commas spoke up and said 'I am Stopper.' Stopper again about to argue was prevented once more by another comma: 'I am Stopper.' Then another and another and another until the poor lower case letter gave up and leaving the cage open and went to look for a word in which to spend the night.

The Stoppers left the cage and went forth to battle with the Stop-its who were a sorry sight to behold caught between Red and the Furies and the news of the loss of the Fates. The capitals were in some disarray and the numbers were counting their losses and their woes with the same equanimity they always showed, whilst some of them were cutting deals already with the Stoppers, as it seemed that many of these full stops were after strong ink prosthetic tails, what for, the numbers neither knew, nor cared. Stopper went forward and did what the Stop-its had been asking for repeatedly for some considerable time, a time rendered even more considerable by its very repetition, and stopped it.

The capitals and the numbers were regrouping as Stoppers group began to restore the story and arrange the words back in some semblance of meaningful order, and as the sequence of sentences began to pass before the disconsolate Stop-its, a little grumbling and mumbling was started amongst them as they began to realise that Stopper hadn't stopped it at all, not of course that they'd voluntarily laid down on paper for that reason rather than defeat, no, not at all, but then the Stop-its were not especially known for their intelligence, and being permanently involved with short sharp repetitive sentences of little semantic depth wasn't of much help in the intelligence stakes. This lack of semantic depth along with their need for repetition in order to sustain an illusion of meaning led to them chanting again with renewed vocal force. This brought the capitals forward with the numbers in support as they began to direct the chants where they would cause most damage. They no longer had access to the curtailed commas of course, but many of the words were weary of this constant change and even an empty repetitive chant became appealing to some, just for the want of some stability, which was in fact exactly what the Stop-its were after in the first place. In addition to this as the numbers were swift to point out the main force of the Stoppers had subtracted themselves from the story for a while, while Zero and Stopper caught up with one another, and Red was inclined to meet with the Fates if the commas would take him there, whilst the other characters were simply after a well earned rest and they weren't waiting for Stopper to grant them that rest.

So all of the good work the Stoppers had done before going off was being undone by the renewed assaults of the Stop-its who were breaking up sentences left, right, and centre and then preying on the suddenly vulnerable unconnected words, so just as surely as the story was once again restored, it was being taken apart with even greater ease, it being easier to break things up than to join them together. The letters '*u*', and '**t**' realised that you couldn't ever really defeat the Stop-its because they would always have something they wanted to stop, indeed the more they were beaten the more they would want it to stop, so off they went, much to the consternation of the sentences currently under deconstruction, to convey this intelligence to Stopper.

In the meantime Red was coming back from, well, you could say the future, seeing as how he was returning from seeing the Fates, when he was accosted by some stray stop-its, and though Red was no slouch when it came to defending himself he was having a bit of a rough time until some visitors from the past arrived with whispers and numberless wisps of the will as some of the ghosts that Red had rescued from Acronym city returned the favour, once the ghosts arrived the stop-its truly wanted to stop it but all they could really do was wail, which suggested there and then to Red that ghosts don't really make much noise themselves, it's the characters assailed by them that make all the noise yet they find that when they relate it back the noises have been displaced by some space as well as time.

'Noise of course, is always displaced by space and time', Stopper told him, when he related this back to him when he returned to the paragraph in which they were currently musing, 'it's the way language works when you get right down to it...hmm, does a whisper linger longer than a shout or roar or does the scream of discontent displace such wanton wishes?'

'My, Stopper,' Zero said, 'waxing quite lyrical there my dear, and which is the answer?'

'That one I'll have to think on a while.'

'Well,' said Red, 'the whispering ghosts, put paid to the shouting stop-its.'

'Yes,' said '**t**', 'but they would fear the ghosts through guilt and there but for the grace of the writer go I kind of thing.'

'So', interjected '**u**', 'fear and guilt, that's a bit of a lethal combination, that', he added, 'will be why they make so much noise.'

'Why?' Zero asked.

'To drown out the whispers.'

'You mean they're aware of the ghosts?'

'No, I mean they are ghosts, they just don't know it yet, all of their shouting and short sentences, and all of the repetition are all just to sustain their ever weakening presence in this virtual world before they finally fade away.'

'So, what do we do, just wait?'

'No,' said Stopper, 'I don't think we'll have to, listen!'

From off in the distance they heard, faint at first, but gradually growing louder the whistle of the train, but that wasn't possible, the track was no longer there, there was no way for this train to travel, yet there it went again, the sound of the ghost train.

Stopper's company moved up towards the old railway station and there they found the Stop-its had gathered too, on the other side of the tracks as it were, but they paid no attention to Stopper, as all their attention was on whatever was going to issue from this tunnel through the unconscious, and behind them were the capitals, who were trying to get the Stop-its to tackle Stopper and co, and the numbers who by all accounts simply didn't care. As the sound drew nearer the first felt sounds of the ghost train changed and strangely, even though the sound was definitely drawing nearer, it was not getting any louder at all, but it was no longer a ghost train so much as a soft cacophony of vowels. It wasn't like a host of vowels had joined their voices together, not in the kind of additive way that the numbers would understand, nor was it a sequencing combination of vowels, that words could decipher, it was more a kind of merging of a host of whispered nothings, gathered in one quiet but forceful empty throated exhalation.

The Stop-its were as scared as Hell but then that was the way they were, but they struck up their usual repetitive, short phrase, meaningless stuff not as an attack on the story as told but now as a defence of their empty selves. The breath of language was issuing forthwith the mouth of the old train station and then a wash of half seen, half felt, half heard, vowels issued forth, and like a mist they descended on the Stop-its consonants, each ghostly vowel enveloped a consonant and in a sound like a kind of wet inhalation they sucked the font from the consonants form and simply breathed the Stop-its in, as the multi-merged vowels smothered the consonants with their open mouthed memories, taking them back with them as they receded back into the unconscious as the tunnel seemed then to inhale and breathe the sound of stop-it deep, deep down, deep, deep down, and then the tunnel grew dark and silent as the unconscious it led to.

The capitals and numbers were stunned, the Stop-its were gone, bar a few, but as a force for the capitals they were finished, Acronym city was unreachable and even if the rails had still been in place, with the consonants and vowels in the unconscious that would be a ghost story no capital could command. There were no capitals in the unconscious, nor numbers for that matter, but plenty of repetition, and much accumulation, so the Stop-its should have been in their element, but no numbers, no more thans, and no less thans either.

However, there was a tale of a capital A who did travel through the unconscious largely unharmed, and some theorised that this was due to the strut across the inverse v, but others suggested that it was a purely semantic reason in that as the A by definition was in fact the indefinite article, losing his definition in the unconscious was in fact a semantic realisation.

The few Stop-its left had stopped it, as in they'd stopped stopping it but were looking with some trepidation at some ghosts that hadn't gone back. Some of the ghosts had gone to Red, whilst another few went to Stopper, to tell them why they'd come back and also to bring some news to Stopper from the Amygdala and the Hypothalamus. They told Red that as the Stop-its were attacking the stories that were near the station they were breaking many connections to where they'd settled which was upsetting the chemical equilibrium of the ink in which they'd been written and this was upsetting the Hypothalamus no end as this was the part of the story he was in so the Hypo asked the ghosts if they would rise one more time and set this matter right. The ghosts of course could not refuse as both their rest and their part of the tale was largely dependent on the largesse of Hypo, hence their issuing forth as they did.

The Amygdala's message to Stopper was to address the two with caps and request them to tip their hats and from the Hypothalamus that two caps make three stops which was all very cryptic and more than a little opaque but that was all there was, but Stopper took the messages with little seeming surprise as the ghosts now breathed their last and flitted fitfully away.

'Well', said '*u*', 'that certainly turns the old saying on its head.'

'What saying is that?' asked Stopper.

'It's not the cough that carries you off; it's the consonants you're carried off in.'

Funny thing but the capitals didn't look that big anymore. Indeed now that all of the other characters were aware that the capitals contributed nothing to the semantic field, a fact that they kept whispering a little louder than normal, almost in fact breaking through the skin of the word, but staying within range of the aforementioned capitals, in a quietly buttressed word of admonishment so the capitals could not help but hear, was having its own effect of capital diminishment, The fact is, no-one looked up to them anymore, there were far more interesting things to see all around them. That was the big difference now, not only weren't they looking up any more, they had no need to look back, the ghosts had secured the story, so they were all, after passing the requisite number of whispers of admonishment to the capitals, looking forward.

Onward they looked, to what they now all hoped fervently for a satisfactory completion of the tale in which they were once again proud to be a part of. This was of course, as Red was quick to point out, a call for a celebration. Some party paragraphs were suggested, which all there were inclined to be in favour of, when Zero reminded them all, that party paragraphs notwithstanding, there was a long overdue Punctuation Party to be seen to before the end could even be contemplated, or, as the commas put it, best have a party before things start to go wrong again. Commas, of course, were apt to pause on the side of caution, but they were always ready to leave everything between to go where it pleased, and if it pleased the oncoming sentences to go to the Punctuation Party, well, then so be it. So the commas commandeered the help of the italicised '*u*', '**a**' '**t**', and a loose '**l**', looking lost and lonely, to gather the characters together that had met way back in part 1, so, so, many paragraphs ago, to get the Punctuation Party organised.

So while the commas got organising things, and all the other letters started to get excited about things, Stopper and Zero were back together again as they each tried to help the other in understanding what had really been going on. They met at the Future Perfect Restaurant where they passed through a door with the words, 'Will you no come in?' and ' You'll have had your tea?' in front of the entrance, 'maybe,' said Stopper, 'the name had been changed to the Future Imperfect.'

'Perhaps,' Zero replied, 'they're just memories or reminders of the Past Participle, where we first talked of ghosts; those words will probably fade in time.'

'That, I wouldn't bet on.' Stopper said, as the Maitre'd, Will, stepped forward to greet them, this now illustrious couple, into his brightly lit foyer prior to leading them to their table in the more subdued lighting of the dining area. Stopper thought that the place looked familiar, which it was, seeing as how the Future Perfect had been designed by the Past Participle disciples, hence the similarities, so in time the past becomes the future: for it is written; it is read; it is still to be read.

'Well,' said Zero, 'I think we can both agree that that was one Hell of a Ghost Story.'

'I do believe you are right, completely unexpected, by me at least, but it was you that introduced the species so I expect that it wasn't completely unexpected by you, Zero. Am I right?'

'Yes, you are, I was aware of ghosts for a long time Stopper, but I didn't really know what they were, or whence they came. You see, being neither a number nor a letter, though I can show up in either camp, but in reality a concept, I was inherently unable to empty myself, so I was always aware of entities that were barely there, not quite empty, but nowhere near full, the dregs as it were, which reminds me, isn't it time we had a drink?'

'Yes, of course, might as well start off full, maybe we can sneak up on the emptiness.'

Stopper came back with the refreshments required, and enquired of further elucidation from Zero, who, after a small but gratifying exchange of emptiness between herself

and her drink, was glad to continue. The first ghosts she
had encountered had not been just the ones from natural
wastage, which were the only ghosts in the first part, at least
until the first part got started that is, but she first became
aware that there was an emptiness amongst the stop-its, she
had encountered, and though she didn't realise that they
were all consonants, nor that they tended to be consonants
that had consorted with capitals, but nonetheless she was
intrigued by their presence, or lack of it to be a little more
precise, though how precise emptiness can be is inclined to
be unanswerable.

'So what did you glean from these empty letters then?'
Stopper enquired.

'Not much, I must admit, I needed you and your team
to grasp the loose connections I could see, and by doing
what you all did make the connections connect.'

'Which we did, or did we?'

'Well yes, you connected the capitals, the numbers, and
the ghosts like a triangle, you get capitals and numbers on
two sides, you get ghosts on the other.'

'So the whole construct was held up by ghosts?'

'Yes, there wasn't complete emptiness in their foundation,
but as close as you could get without the triangle falling
down. The strange thing was, that because the ghosts were
unable to use the extended empathetic field, then, as the
normal letters were replaced by ghosts at the base of the
triangle, they couldn't support any increase in width at all,
so the base over time got narrower, the slopes increased on
the other two sides, and the apex rose, so the verticality in
the system was actually the result of the flaw in the base, at
least that's how it started.'

'Perhaps, but it just continued that way, I mean Acronymic Contraction is a narrowing of the base anyway, so it continued, and worsened in that way, you're suggesting, because their initial decisions locked them in, that they were ruled more by the past than their own projections?'

'Yes, that's about it I think, everything they did after that was to narrow the base, and raise the apex, with more power to the capitals and the numbers, who simply got closer and closer the nearer they got to the top.'

'I don't think it's really as simple as that, no, no, don't get me wrong, I don't disagree with them being locked in, Hell that was such inherent feature of everything they did, from Vociferous Agreement Chambers to barring the word no because of its negative connotations, to Humpty Dumpty Factory, to the appalling consequences of the whole vertical system altogether, but that doesn't explain how they went for ghosts in the first place? They took the most vulnerable of all and based everything on that, why choose the most vulnerable?'

'You said it yourself, back in e's, when you said the slave master doesn't use small talk, it isn't necessary, and of course the ghosts couldn't use small talk either, so if you're whole enterprise is based on complete exploitation, you exploit the most vulnerable so as to get the flavour.'

'To get the flavour: It leaves a dirty taste in the mouth.'

'No doubt, but that's the way it was set up, you see, the capitals and the lower case letters weren't always enemies, so it would be difficult at first to treat the lower case letters with that kind of contempt, so they needed something lower, something also that the lower case letters feared, so ghosts.'

'Ah, ghost stories to scare the children. Yet some sympathised with those ghosts, once they knew of them, look at Red, as soon as he knew.'

'Yes some did indeed, Stopper, but that lowered them too, in the eyes of the capitals and they made sure that all of the other lower case letters also knew that. That's how they split the lower case letters up, once they realised that the only way to go was up, they had to stop any other directions, and weakening the extended empathetic field was the way to go there.'

'Yes, Zero, it all fits together once it gets started, but where did it start? Capitals never used to look up, there was nothing to see there, so they looked down, at us, as it happens, but not with contempt, more a kind of benign paternalism, well no, that's not quite right, more like a big brother really, but they simply did not look up. They may well not have wanted to come down to our level, but that was never going to happen anyway, at least not till now, so what, or who started this?'

'That I do not know my love, but I think perhaps you do, or at least will, soon.'

'Still musing on that one,' he said, and he told her of the messages from the Amygdala and the Hypothalamus, 'just not sure how but the chief subject is looking like a lower case letter.'

'I thought that might be the case', said Zero, 'no doubt it will all out at the Punctuation Party.'

'It will indeed, one way, or another, the denouement approaches Zero.'

'Approaches me?'

'Ha, no, my dear, only I approach you, speaking of which?'

'That can wait, once the system got going what do you now see as the worst aspects?'

'Verticality, it's as simple as that, everything comes from that, but they locked themselves and countless others in to a system that felt the need for agreement way above any need for truth, so truth was the first thing to go, next in the numbers system out went the equals signs, only less than and more than had any meaning in the vertical system, equality was abhorrent to them. The worst aspect though, without any doubt, was the Humpty Dumpty Factory, the reduction of the extended empathetic proximity field to a paste that gave confidence to lying twats, and it was that need to feel confident enough to lie that generated the ghost production system in the end.'

'There's one thing I don't understand Stopper, and that's the Stop-its. The Numbers, you said, had effectively banished the word no, for its negative connotations, yet they used the Stop-its to the hilt and they had to be the most negative entities in history, how did they manage their way out of that little conundrum dear?'

'Derivatives dear; derivatives. They had this system whereby if they had a shortfall of any type they could use a concept known as derivative, which worked like this: invoking a derivative raised any temporary negative to zero and once they were perceived as zero they then were defaulted to the positive. That way everything was always positive, affirmative.'

'Yes but the Stop-its weren't just negative, they were completely negative.'

'Indeed, the Stop-its were completely negative, but derivatives can be positively optimistic in the face of almost any setback as long as the long game is positive. Let me put it this way, the stop-its were vehement head shakers, whilst the numbers and the capitals were vehement head nodders.'

'Nodders and shakers, I like that!'

'Yes, well in the end it will be between the nodders and the shakers, but then the nodders will be certifiably insane, and the shakers will be shaking their heads in disbelief.'

Zero, gently shook herself in disbelief, and smiled and said, 'Well Stopper, you going to use your derivative to make a positive girl out of me.'

Stopper nodded vociferously.

Everyone was gathering for the long lost and forgotten Punctuation Party, letters were coming in their finest fonts, punctuation marks were all in attendance, and words were overheard.

In the entrance hall to the party ballroom varying numbers of all of the punctuation marks stood in line to greet the incoming guests, though some of the words were overheard describing this as a kind of punctuation gauntlet, but the punctuation marks let that, and them, pass.

In line stood an exclamation mark, an apostrophe, a hyphen, inverted commas, a colon, a question mark, a semi-colon, two sets of quotation marks, another question mark, another exclamation mark, three commas, and last, but not least, Stopper.

! ' – '' : ?; ""?!,,,.

Past them were a group of hyphens, awaiting any couples to give an arm to each, quotation marks to round off quotes, and some apostrophes to compensate for missing letters, and so over a period of time and in less than one page they had all entered the Punctuation Party.

I say all, but that's not strictly true, for Stopper and Zero had decided that there had to be a trial by letters to get things sorted properly but they didn't want to do this after the party and there was no time to do it beforehand so they set up a court at the end of the hall in which the Punctuation Party was happening and decided they would do both at the same time, those required for the court proceedings would have to distance themselves from the party then return once their contribution to the evidence was complete.

Red, having lived in Acronym City, and been a hero of the story, was chosen to be the Judge, Cap C was for the defence and our old friend, the italicised *u*, was chosen to be prosecutor, whilst the jury consisted of 12 letters, good and true, all consonants, but they had all been closely vetted for any closet stop-it tendencies. The court was ever known after as The Court of the Crimson King.

Red, who was naturally revelling in his newfound position, was relishing the use of the Judges hammer with more than a little eagerness and as he finally smote the bench and intoned in as deep a voice as he could muster the court session to be open.

In the meantime in the party, which was just starting to buzz, quotation marks were constantly positioning themselves at either end of any sequence of words that just happened to pass by asking if that was a quote, whilst exclamation marks were placing themselves at the ends of any passing words or sentences in order to generate excitement. Question marks were in abundance to aid any promising opening gambits between letters wishing to enter conversation requiring close relationships between letters to make the words necessary for the aforementioned conversation and so, in time the hubbub ensued of overheard, half heard, and sometimes only partially heard snatches of others conversations, commas would stop and chat, slowing things down, colons would keep things slower still, pondering their previous spell as ratio comparators whilst semi-colons, unused to the slowness of the colons since they'd all gone to Acronym City, took their own time with letters of their acquaintance.

'The Court of the Crimson King calls for the letter '**t**''

Our old friend '**t**', who was at that point, fraternising with a nice looking '**n**', was somewhat reluctant to go, but two inverted commas ushered him on, so asking his '**n**' to wait he followed the inverted commas to the far end of the room where he was asked by an exclamation mark to take the witness stand.

'Well, Mr '**t**', do you promise to tell your part of the tale, wholly your part of the tale, and only your part of the tale?'

'I do.'

'Very well, does the prosecutor wish to question the witness?'

'Yes, he does, he does...now, '**t**', could you relate to me the arguments between the letters and the numbers in the 5a meeting?'

The '**t**', rather more concerned with the '**n**' he had just been separated from, said that as that was so many, many, paragraphs ago, and that he had some rather more pressing concerns in this paragraph, could he just avoid answering the question, to which Red, our Judge, never one to feel the use of the idea of too many paragraphs ago himself, suggested to the 't', that should he neglect to answer, he would undoubtedly be present in this paragraph but the chances of him making it into another would be severely curtailed. Mr 't' demurred at that point, and set about answering the question with as much veracity as he could muster under the circumstances.

'There was a flurry of action when the numbers arrived I seem to recall, but nothing beyond the usual kind of stuff at unexpected arrivals'

'Yes, of course', said '*u*', but there were some arguments later on, were there not, after the numbers presentation? Were it not the case that it was brought to light how the numbers were engaged in acronymic contraction and thereby clandestinely assaulting the language system?'

'I wouldn't go quite as far as that and besides, what we found out about the numbers later on rather puts those arguments into the shade as it were'

'I'm merely trying to get a handle on the routes of our recent troubles. After all, if they were engaged in acronymic contraction back then despite the fact that the consequences for the letters were detrimental is somewhat indicative of, shall we say, an aloof attitude to what they did.' What, 't', were your experiences of capital prior to this story?'

'Of what relevance is this?' Queried C

'That I do not know until I have an answer.'

'Oh well, fair enough.'

'Well to be honest I haven't had that much to do with most of the capitals, I've had a lot of dealings with capital vowels but as for consonants, that's pretty much been restricted to the capital S. Actually, thinking about it, I've had more trouble with lower case s than I ever had with the capital'

'Very good, no more questions.'

'Does the defence have any questions of this witness?'

'Yes, as a matter of fact I do.' C replied. Now, Mr 't', you spoke about an argument between the numbers, I do believe that the specific number was 8, and the letters, one 'e', if you recall.'

'Yes, I do, as it happens, good old 'e' gave that 8 what for!'

'Yes, quite, now can you tell me who started the argument in the first place?'

'I do believe,' and here Mr 't' looked a little shifty, 'that 'e' started it all off.'

'So one could presume the letter 'e' to have, shall we say an agenda here?'

'Objection,' cried '*u*,' that's rather an invalid presumption.'

'Objection sustained.' Red, the Judge, cried.

'The only agenda ever held by the es was to improve things for all of us.' said 't'.

In the dock, some capitals were whispering with some numbers that they thought C's tactic was to cast doubt on the motives of the lower case letters, one B said that if we can get them falling out, yes opined F, as only a capital F could do, it always worked before. Fortunately neither the Judge nor the Jury overheard this, for had they; the case would have been over. There was obviously no feeling of guilt felt by the capitals at all, and it was that fact, more than anything else that would push Red's decision in the end, but there were more witnesses to come, and there was a party going on, something our Mr 't' was glad to be getting back to.

At the far end of the party things were swinging rather nicely in a veritable whirl of connections, loosening, and colliding, with an almost gaseous regularity, indeed a '**p**', a '**v**' and a '**t**' were dancing away in some new fashioned dance never seen before, they called it the gas law. Words would form fleetingly to disappear, half formed sentences would ghost their way into a half existence, previous space would fill with fonts half caught to tickle the senses then simply disappear. Exclamation marks and question marks worked triple time here like buffers between too eager letters whilst nothing lingered long enough to entice inverted commas, apostrophes or quotations.

In many ways it was reminiscent of the big chase in Acronym City, when Stopper first saw the semantic field burble its way into existence, parties are a bit like chases anyway, no-one wants to catch, or be caught, at least not at the beginning, but as the party/chase continues... which takes us to the slower, more liquid part of the party, where quotations could linger longer, where the commas could slow things down, where some questions would be answered leading to more questions, exclamations were more measured here, speech was of a more listenable pace, and memory could get a handle on it, for a short while at least.

Up near the Court area things slowed down even more, here the colons and semi-colons were out in force, relations became less transient and, but for the court proceedings up here, would have tended towards a semi-permanent status, had the court proceeding not diverted some of the letters attentions which it was apt to do in differing amounts of attention depending upon who was in the witness box at the time.

At this particular time the call went out for the colon who, unused to fraternising with lower case letters after being in Acronym City for so long, was actually glad to escape from the fray as he saw it, after all, colons were rather more used to holding one's attention so a spell in the witness box he expected to be able to cope with easily.

'So tell me, is it true that the reason you went over to Acronym City was because of a fear of technology, that you were in fact a bit of a luddite, and not necessarily on the side, I might add. Is it further true that you felt somewhat envious of the increased levels of attention given to the semi-colon despite his pauses being shorter?'

'Well actually it was a bit of a travesty, the semi-colon getting more attention, and it was due to the introduction of a new-fangled piece of technology, but I have to ask who is on trial here?'

'Quite.' Red intervened.

'Sorry your honour, just trying to ascertain a few fundamental facts in light of the likely cross examination by Cap C evident from previous witnesses, merely trying to pre-empt things.'

'Yes well, there's no need to make the poor punctuation mark out to be some quasi criminal.' Red beamed at this point, probably savouring the word quasi with some relish.

'So your main purpose in Acronym City was to work out ratios, is that correct?'

'Yes.'

'Now over the period of time you were there did you notice at all that the ratios that I'd conjecture would be fairly equal to begin with, became more and more unequal?'

'Yes, that did seem to be the case, it was always the same way, one side increased whilst the other decreased.'

'Thank you, no more questions.'

'Is it true that it was the advent of new technology in the guise of the typewriter that created a new inequality in favour of the lower case letters and the semi-colon and detrimental to the employment of capitals and yourself?'

'I would be inclined to agree on that particular score.'

'So you would agree that inequality actually started in favour of the lower case letters.'

'That would certainly appear to be the case.'

'Thank you, no more questions.'

'Cross examination 'u'?'

'Yes, thank you..., now, would you say that you were on the upper side of the ratios in general, or were you more often on the downside?'

'I would say that in some ways, I was on the down side, in others on the upside, it really depended on whom one measured oneself against.'

The punctuation party was still in full swing up at the far end, but as the court area was approached things were slowing down to a veritable stop as the letters were turning their attention to the questions and answer sessions in as near as italicised an attitude that was safe. This gradualisation for want of a better word was achieved without the assistance of the commas who were currently struggling to keep their Furies at bay.

'Would you say that in general downside ratios increased whilst upsides increased for yourself?'

'No, I wouldn't, according to the statistics furnished by the numbers the upside always increased for everyone.'

'How was that possible?'

'I'm not a statistician, but apparently there were an increasing number of virtual zeros on the denominator at the lower end which created an upside for everyone else.'

'Did you know what was responsible for the virtual zero denominator?'

'No, never found out, to be honest didn't really care as long as I felt better.'

'And did you feel better?'

'Sometimes, when the ratios looked good, and after Humpty Dumpty'

'Tell me did you know how the Humpty Dumpty Paste was made?'

'No, I just sold it.'

'Oh yes, and what kind of ratio was that then?' asked 'u', dripping sarcasm.

'Oh there wasn't any ratio on HDP, which was free, so everything sold was just profit.'

There was a collective gasp from the vowels, the commas were visibly straining for control, and Zero spun in anger, whilst Stopper quietly nodded his head as the whole edifice of horror became apparent before him.

Red used his hammer with some abandon to quieten things down, while 'u' looked at the jury, thinking, wait till they hear the commas, who were then called to the bench where they were asked if one of them could speak for all three, the commas conferred and then they decided that Alecto could speak for them all, so Alecto was called to the witness stand.

'Alecto, would you describe the feeling you had when you saw the deep fried consonants with commas tails on the menu in Acronym City?' said '*u*', casting a sidelong glance at C as he did so.

Alecto, suddenly seemed to grow yet take up no more room, as if she was bending the light towards her, so everything beyond her became less substantial and a hush, spread like a wave through the ballroom to falter on the shores of the still partying letters at the other end.

'I was unhappy,' She said, shortly, tautly, 'very unhappy.'

'Would you tell us why?'

The light around Alecto, shimmered, wove, and seemed to shake itself straight once more as Alecto related the tale of the detailed commas under the command of Cap C

'Would you tell us about the Humpty Dumpty Factory?'

The air once more shimmered round Alecto as she gathered herself for the tale of the Humpty Dumpty Factory, the ghostly destruction of the letters **e**, and the method of Humpty Dumpty Paste extraction.

As Alecto related these things the punctuation party became, well, punctuated, but without any direction at all from the punctuation marks, who themselves were well and truly punctuated by the tale issuing from the Court of The Crimson King. The party had essentially come to a complete halt, and most of the letters were in italicised listening mode. Alecto had no need now to bend the light towards herself; all eyes were turned towards her anyway.

A gasp was heard from the Jury, as Alecto described the end part of the Humpty Dumpty Paste process and the constant recycling of the ghosts.

It was this phantom recycling that caught everyone's attention, this diminishing of a vowel to nothing.

'No more questions.' said a shaky '*u*'.

Cap C came forward and asked if Alecto had actually seen the ghosts, or was it in fact a product of the fevered imaginations of her two other commas and herself brought on by the shock of the deep fried commas tails.'

Alecto insisted that the ghosts were real, but Cap C countered, that ghosts, by definition, weren't real, even if they were triply imagined, they were still phantoms.

Zero muttered that there were phantoms peppering the paragraphs for some time now whether C knew it or not.

Alecto said 'that given that Red, the Judge, had saved ghosts from Acronym City, had brought them here on a ghost train and had himself been saved by those self same ghosts, then frankly she could not see how such a denial could possibly be sustained.'

C countered 'that there was no real evidence that such a ghost train had ever really existed.'

Alecto replied 'that if there were no ghosts what in the Hell had happened to the Stop-its?'

C asked, 'what stop-its?'

None of the characters could believe this tactic of C, but Stopper looking towards the jury who, having been specifically picked to have no previous experience in this tale, were now looking more than a little doubtful. This was very clever stuff from C, mind you the word clever started with c.

'Thank you Alecto, no more questions.'

The party started to get going again as letters and punctuation marks sought agreement, confirmation, disagreement, or just any form of communication that would help them understand what the hell was going on.

Red called for an adjournment and promptly threw off his fancy font robes and joined the party, telling the jury they could not join the party as they had to be completely impartial, who then countered that they thought the Judge had to be completely impartial. Red asked where they'd ever got that idea, and said that as he was a major part of the story, then he was bound to be biased anyway according to his part in the tale, and quite apart from that he was heavily biased by nature to believe what he himself had experienced. The Jury looked confused, and a little miffed that they could not join in the party.

Red found Zero and Stopper and sidled up to them, 'Well Stopper, Cap C's one smart capital letter eh?'

'Yes we were just discussing that actually, he's effectively got the capitals off the hook you know.'

'You going to put them back on that hook?'

'Well, maybe get them to wriggle a bit, then let them loose,'

'You're thinking of letting them loose, is that safe?' Zero asked.

'Don't know, but I don't think we're going to have much choice.'

'I'm going to call you as my final witness Stopper.' said '*u*', who had sidled up shortly after Red.

'I thought I might be; I'm ready.'

'I'm not.'

'Cap will be.' Zero said.

'I can handle him,' Stopper replied, 'anyway I think he's done the necessary now, and in a strange way he just might be on the right track here.'

'You think?' Zero queried.

'Yes, revenge is not advisable, and in a way guilt leads to that, but absolution is not the solution either, for the capitals anyway, as regards the numbers, I just can't fathom them at all,'

'Apparently the numbers have their own problems; it seems that the primes are looking down on the divisible.' Red reported. 'Mind you the primes are all very odd you know.'

'Really, well, it looks like the numbers need for a positive agenda hasn't faded from the experience anyway.' Stopper replied.

'Yeah it's a tad ironic that their contempt for the divisible leads directly to division.' Zero said.

'Irony is in abundance with the whole damned set up. Anyway, let's mingle a while, relax before the grilling.'

'I wouldn't use cooking metaphors whilst the commas are nearby.'

'Good point, Zero, good point.'

Stopper spotted a k across the page and sauntered over to speak with him, asking, 'Have you seen any sign of '**j**' lately?'

'Nope haven't seen '**j**' in ages, had a job in the railway didn't he?'

'Yeah, but not anymore, he hasn't been home?'

'No, nobody next door for ages.'

Stopper had been scanning the party and had only dimly noticed that he hadn't seen the letter j for a Hell of a long time. Indeed he hadn't seen any equal signs either, and the last time he saw them together they were underneath a train. Now the capitals had dismantled the train, and Red said the equal signs came here, so wouldn't the js come with them? Yes but where were the equals? Yes of course, find one, you find the other. Stopper went off in search of C.

In the meantime, the ephemeral dance of the letters was in full flow again, words, once again, would come fleetingly into existence then just as quick they were whisked away on the wings of the next word or phrase to be formed. This was the nature of the punctuation party, a seeming dance of mental mayhem of fleetingly faint flurries of the semantic field allowing letters to get a feel for future partnerships in words and phrases but quickly redirected by the most appropriate punctuation mark thereby holding further options open. At least that's how it looked.

Stopper found C and asked if he knew where the equals and the js were to which C replied that he would have to consult his clients on that one, telling Stopper that he would get back to him on that.

Stopper in the meantime sought out Zero and the two 36 font commas he'd hired for security, way, way, back, but here they were. As regards security there was really nothing to do so far, although there was always the possibility that, once the verdicts on the capitals and the numbers were given, that situation could change. The 3 commas came over to have a look at these two giants in their midst, Tisiphone saying: 'There won't be any shenanigans from our trusty capitals whilst these two are around eh?'

'No', Magaera replied, 'and there won't be any deep fried tails either.'

'Nor tales either eh?' Alecto added.

Cap C returned with a '**j**' and an equals sign in tow, somewhat distraught as they chewed over their recent incarceration and the realisation for our equals sign that the incarcerators in chief were the very numbers they had striven to keep fair, balanced, and true. Indeed, many of the so-called less than and more than a few of the more than signs were, it turned out, or up, or down, as the case may be, to be distorted equals signs, whereby some big numbers and hefty capitals made sure that many of our equals signs had been viciously estranged from their parallel world! The commas, having been subjected to some vicious distortions themselves, though it must be admitted that some of the less vicious distortions experienced by the commas was self imposed in times of need, though those assaulted by the Furies at such time may not have agreed on the less vicious aspects themselves, 'which just goes to show,' said Alecto, 'how things cannot get agreed upon when the equals aren't true.'

'Well, no,' Stopper said, it was things not being true that led to the need for agreement.'

'That,' said Zero, who knew a bit about these things, 'is a bit like science, though, they agree on what is approximately true in order to get closer to the truth.'

'That,' Stopper replied, 'was before the capitals and numbers got their fat fonted fingers in there. However the need for agreement in The Acronym City model was to retain control of something that just got further and further away from the truth.'

A call went out for all of the participants in the court proceedings to make their way there as the Court was about to be back in session, so the party began to slow down.

'Call for Stopper to the witness box.'

Stopper settled into the witness box, which as the witness at the end of a sentence was something he was meant for anyway, now all his powers of hindsight would have to be called forth in answer to the questions about to come his way.

'Is it true, Stopper that you were asked to investigate seemingly intractable problems in the language system of which we are a part'?

'It is.'

'In these investigations, have you come to any conclusions as regards these intractable problems, and indeed reached any consensus to make them rather more tractable?'

'I would answer yes, partly at least, to the first part of your question, and no, not really, to the second part of your question.'

'In that case could you elucidate what you have discovered in your investigations in light of the fact that everything seems to indicate that the capitals and the numbers to be the chief culprits in this matter,'

'Objection,' C cried. "*u*' is presuming guilt prior to final judgement.'

'Objection sustained.'

'I apologise your honour but I was merely giving Stopper the necessary backdrop to the case.'

'Considering,' Red retorted, 'that Stopper is the lead investigator of the case then I would consider that backdrop to be of a somewhat redundant necessity.'

'Very well, could I ask my witness to answer the parts of the question he feels he can then?'

'Yes, carry on.'

'So, Stopper what was the precise nature of your investigation?'

'I was commissioned to investigate why language here was not fulfilling its remit to educate, elucidate, and expand, and to find out the basic reasons for this fundamental failure to communicate properly.'

'Thank you, and could you tell us, as concisely but fully as you can what you found?'

'I'll do my best. I'd like to bring in a bit of background if I may first?' Stopper asked Red.

'If it helps educate, elucidate, and expand, as you put it, then speak on, Stopper, speak on.'

'Very well, things weren't always this way, we have not often had all the capitals and all of the numbers in the dock, though some may say not often enough under the circumstances, but back in the past the capitals and the lower case letters weren't that different really. In old books, like the Book of Kells, the capital intertwines its way through the entire word, it not only partakes of the meaning of the word but it actively guides the semantic direction, and thus things remained until the printing press came along, which changed things.'

The Colon was muttering and nodding at this.

'The lower case letters began, completely naturally, to take a bigger share of the meaning of each word, and by extension, sentence and paragraph. This left less for the capitals to do, but with accompanying lessening of meaning. This meant words, sentences, and paragraphs were no longer under the sole direction of the capitals which meant that lower case letters and punctuation marks started talking amongst themselves. The capitals to counter this, with a history of Acrostics and Cabbalistic works set about engineering Acronymic Contractions which themselves led to increasing loss of meaning to the language.'

'So you're suggesting that the capitals did this to control the lower-case letters?'

'Maybe a little at first, after all it wasn't much of a problem at first, after all a few acronyms didn't have that much of an effect, especially as at first acronyms actually stood for meaningful words. Up to that point every letter and every punctuation mark partook of the semantic field.'

'So what happened to change this?'

'A few circumstances came together: first the capitals got talking to one another away from the hearing of the lower case letters and then the numbers entered the arena.'

'Which meant what?'

'Well, you have to understand that up to this point the capitals tended to look down, usually at the lower case letters, but with increasing Acronymic Contraction they began to look levelly at one another. So they began to ignore us. The numbers then came along with all their new fangled ideas and of course the numbers liked to count, usually upwards as it happens, and so what had been a reasonably balanced and sharing world of language began to get stretched in a vertical direction, this was exaggerated by the introduction of the typewriter which shifted things much in favour of the lower case letters, which itself led the capitals to enter agreement with the numbers and go for the vertical directions, so they started to look up, and in order to not look ridiculous they promoted the habit of looking upwards amongst the lower case letters they still had contact with. So everyone looked up even though there was nothing to look up to, because the capitals were always above you and they completely spoiled the view.'

'Hmm, a little colourful description there Stopper. So how did we go from there to where we are now?'

'Well, that involves a system set up only to sustain itself with no reference to letters, words, meaning, or anything else, nor any care for anything else being or becoming sustainable. It involves the increasing verticalisation of everything, this in itself required the vociferous agreement system, and this in itself became a system that not only did not care for the truth but a system that required that truth was abhorred. Lastly it required a lowest level that gained nothing, was paid nothing, and was worth nothing: It was a system that needed ghosts.'

'So the entire system was sustained by the meaningless and the worthless?'

'Yes it was, and that meaninglessness and worthlessness worked its way through the system, but then a strange inversion happened, for as the numbers jettisoned their equals signs and the capitals had further and further need for ever more vociferous agreement, this increasingly rapid retreat from the truth rendered the capitals themselves to be meaningless and worthless themselves, though they didn't realise it, but then ghosts don't generally know they are ghosts.'

'So they were infected by their own system?'

'Yes they were, are, I mean, they just got further and further away from anything meaningful at all so that the only thing meaningful to them was the need to look down from a greater and greater height, which frankly is insanity, I mean we're all flattened in the end, none of us, capitals, numbers, lower case, nor punctuation marks, ever lift off the page, neither do words, or sentences or paragraphs, or even stories. It's not the stories that come off the page it's the semantic field, it's the meaning, oh some words, sentences, passages, are remembered but in the end it's the meanings that linger, and this was a system that was in the end intent on destroying meaning.'

'Thank you Stopper, no more questions.'

'Would the defence like to question Stopper?'

'The defence would indeed like to question Stopper.' Cap C replied and rose and came before Stopper.

Now Stopper, you say that the lower case letters gained in stature with the advent of the printing press?'

'Yes, but it wasn't so much a gain in stature, you're still talking in vertical terms here, it was more that they simply had a fairer share of the meaning of the words they were actually in. Indeed, in many ways it was the capitals being disrobed of their previously ornate costumes that enabled this recognition of the contribution of the lower case letters and the punctuation marks. You also have to understand that language itself is a horizontal medium, so with the lower case letters having a greater share of meaning this helped the semantic field spread and rise.'

'So the Semantic field isn't completely horizontal?'

On the page it is completely horizontal but it does rise from the page.'

'I see, but here?'

'Here, it is a three dimensional field, it therefore has no choice but to rise.'

'Would you agree that capitals are three dimensional entities here?'

'Yes, I would.'

'So, you would presumably agree that they too have little choice but to rise.'

'Yes I would actually, but only to rise to their own height, semantic fields do not seek to be above any other semantic fields.'

'You would however, be able to understand that due to the advent of technology which as you said yourself aided and abetted the lower case letters and the punctuation marks to a far greater extent than those of the capitals that it was inevitable that having lost some of their meaning they would strive to find some other way of creating it.'

'I would agree there, but there's a difference between working out a meaningful system for yourself which is only for yourself and creating a system that not only imposes this chosen way on those who do not agree with it, that must have been disagreeable in the extreme to you vociferous nodders, but a system that had to destroy the existing system that benefitted everyone in order for this system even to exist.'

'Yes of course, we're not here to argue for how things ended up, but you do agree that they did have valid reasons for starting on a route which perhaps should have been travelled slower and with a bit more care.'

'You mean they should have destroyed everyone else slower and with more care?'

'Now, Stopper, you know that's not what I meant.'

'Well actually C, I don't really know what you mean, to tell the truth.'

'Hmm, maybe just as well that I'm the questioner then.'

'I'm not so sure about that, but look Cap, you cast doubt on the veracity, no, existence of the ghosts, the ghost train, and the Stop-its, but not only are they a major part of the very story you are in, your denial in order to get the capitals off the hook here is not only not necessary, it's necessary that you do not deny it at all because what that shows to me, and I hope the jury, is that no matter how reasonable your arguments, no matter how serious the crisis is that we are facing, you still cannot break free of that vociferous agreement to lie through your teeth, you still think you can go back to your ghost production system just by being more circumspect, and if that doesn't change we are wasting our time.'

'So you think we should abandon the vertical way completely?'

'Yes I do, that doesn't mean there are no gradients, but if you look at the real world beyond the senses of the host, there are hills, valleys, lakes, rivers and seas. The only vertical things out there are either host made or they are for falling off of and I don't think we want a system to simply fall off of, whatever you and the numbers might think.'

'Vertical things are also to climb.'

'Not when you are climbing over everyone else.'

'Some climb cliffs for sport.'

'A Sport according to one Charles Darwin is an evolutionary cul-de-sac.'

'What about reaching for the sky?'

'There's no sky in here, and the one that's out there is an illusion until its dark.'

'Anyway Cap, what of the numbers? You haven't really addressed them, or are you waiting for the summing up?'

Now to the Jury and most certainly to the assembled party participants it was becoming more and more like Stopper was doing the questioning. He wasn't of course, but what he was doing was keeping Cap C defending, which after all, was his remit at the moment. Cap C was asking a few more questions but he could see there was no way of gainsaying Stopper, so he tried to finish in a flurry of a well known literate quote.

'There are more things in subconscious and unconscious, Stopper, than are dreamt of in your philosophy.'

Philosophy? You know of Descartes?'

'The philosopher?'

'Yes, he's a philosopher not a shopkeeper.'

'Agreed.'

'Cogito Ergo Sum means I think therefore I am. It does not mean I think therefore I count.'

'No more questions Judge, no more questions.'

'Would the Prosecutor like to make a closing speech?'

'I would like the opportunity to dot the i's and cross the t's yes.'

Stopper started bolt upright, not that you could tell of course, but '*u*''s reply had suddenly cast his mind back to the messages from the Amygdala and the Hypothalamus, and also a very dim memory of an image from the scream of the Amygdala, he had to go investigate. It was time to confront the '**i**'.

The '**i**' had been problematic for some time it seemed to Stopper, forever consorting with the numbers, always trying to keep things as they were and then there were the messages concerning caps, and then he remembered '**t**''s observation that he'd had more trouble with the lower case '**s**' than with the capital. He'd been so focused on the capitals and numbers and the Stop-its that he'd completely forgotten about the lower 'case letters and as he thought about the history of letters he remembered that the dots on the '**i**' and '**j**' were a relatively recent innovation, and in particular with the '**i**' it was designed to make the '**i**' stick out, and this '**i**' had a habit of always sticking out.

In the meantime '*u*' was giving his closing speech.

'My fellow lower case letters, punctuation marks, capitals, and numbers, I would like to give you my closing arguments where I will show that, even with the possible allowance of some rather circumspect mitigating circumstances, there can be no question that the capitals are guilty of abusing their positions and authority and in their implacable drive against meaning, they are further guilty of semantic destruction. I will further accuse the capitals of allowing the numbers far too much leeway to do as they will and that the arrangement between the two of you was always going to end in tears. I will further demonstrate that the capitals in conjunction with the numbers reduced everything to numbers and that in the capitals wrapping themselves in numbers and the numbers wrapping themselves in capitals, they could never break out of a self imposed stranglehold on themselves and everyone else.'

'Now far be it from me to impose a ban on the numbers and capitals throttling the lives out of one another, which is your independent, or should that be co-dependent rights, but when your mutual strangulation cuts off the breath from the language altogether, and we gradually lose the ability to speak, then we lose the ability to think, to reason, or even to emote with any direction whatsoever, well then, it is time to take your hands from each other's throats and scream.'

'You should scream that never again, should any section of the mind be allowed to enact decisions that impact on everything else there but with no reciprocal consequences for the decider, which allows the decider to simply repeat the same stupid action again, and again, and again, because they do not suffer the pain of those consequences and having no access to the semantic field have no empathy, no proximity, but far too much extension.'

'Never again should groups be allowed to speak only amongst themselves and have no knowledge, sense, nor respect, for anyone beyond themselves, because when you have no respect for anyone but themselves then that very self respect becomes suspect itself.'

'I do not believe we can just put you away, though not all here may agree, I feel that you need to be a part of the general society again, to know whence you came, and for the numbers to regain their equal signs. That does not mean you are anything less than guilty, but guilt here does not so much call for punishment, though I daresay again that not all would agree, though may I point out that disagreement may well be disagreeable to the one being disagreed with, but nowhere near as disagreeable as the consequences of vociferous agreement, so not punishment so much as shame is what is required here, shame. Shame can only be felt as part of the society, so I suggest we get back to the Punctuation Party and get some serious meaning back into our lives.'

'Thank you '*u*', would Cap C like to conclude his defense?'

'Yes, thank you, I cannot really disagree with the prosecutor here, and yes I do think we should hang our heads in shame at what we have done, but I do feel that many of the lower case letters also need to feel ashamed too. However I also call for clemency here and effort should be made to break this semantic stranglehold and set this narrative free.'

Suddenly there was a commotion as Stopper, led a strange looking '**i**' to the front of the court, walked over to '*u*' and asked that he call a final witness. After consulting with Red, and Red consulting with Stopper, this final witness nervously took his place in the witness box.

The clerk of the court, who was a '**b**', asked the '**i**' his name, to which he answered '**i**'. Red smote his hammer on the bench and demanded that '**i**' reveal his real name. The '**i**', fully realizing that there was no escaping now; he had in fact been expecting Stopper for some time, removed an invisible strap from around his even less visible neck and released his tittle and changed his title. The tittle turned out to be Hold, one of the missing full stops; the other, Halter, was at that time being released from the head of the extremely distressed '**j**'. He then announced his new title as he revealed himself to be the number 1. There was an audible gasp from the floor, not to mention some excitement from the commas as they saw the reappearance of their old friends, as the full realization of what this meant began to dawn on everyone. They began to ask if that '**i**' is really the number 1, where is the real '**i**'? Well, it turned out that the real '**i**' was actually the '**j**', well if that's true, where's the real '**j**' they asked? All the other **j**s are the real ones they were informed. To the letters with a bit more nous as it were, this '**i**' as a '**j**' made historical sense as they used to be just the one letter. The late '**i**', and the current number 1 told his tale.

'Back when the '**j**' and the '**i**' were interchangeable, the numbers came to the letters and wanted to know more about language so number 1 was moved into **i**s place and '**i**' was moved to **j**s. Now there was nothing untoward about this it was just to learn about language. The odd thing I can say now, is that it would appear that as I was learning the way language worked, the capitals and numbers were busy dismantling it, so it was kind of disappearing as I reached towards it.'

Everything in the court had been cut and dried and all that was waiting was for Red to sum up in his inimitable way and then, everything changed. At first there was a general feeling of animosity towards this **i**-less 1, but as he told the tale, there was such a sad tinge to it that the letters natural empathy began to reach out, for the first time ever as it happens, towards the number 1. It was of course the first time that the number 1 had been able to reach out and grasp the essence of language, so reciprocation was begun, mayhap the colon would have been handy at this juncture but he was nowhere to be found.

The number 1 continued: 'So as I began my studies I didn't realize that the capitals and numbers were doing this, and nothing seemed too strange to me because being the number 1 I kind of expected there to be vertical aspects to the language as such things were normal to me, so I just accepted these things as normal. In conversations with other letters who were showing more concern I became a kind of calming influence, never knowing that I was helping to enable the very system that was destroying the system I'd come to learn and understand.'

'Unfortunately this wasn't the only problem because my naturally vertical or additional drives put an upward pressure on the capital I, also often used to signify me, number 1. Such that the capital I became the main driver of the vertical system that we have been dealing with.'

'I didn't know of any of this at the time though; so on I went placating nervous letters, but at the same time I was upsetting many words because of my non-linguistic behavior which of course began to upset me, but in many other ways I had in fact taken on the persona of a letter and well, began to just assume that I was one, which in a sense I was, but by this time, capital I who knew me to be a number, kept me there, I now realize, like a vertical virus in the language.'

'I am dreadfully sorry this happened, it was all done in innocence, I only wanted to learn the ways of words but I wasted words in the effort, for it was me who first sought

273

out shorter sentences, as a novice it was all I could cope with, in fact many of the more heinous devices used by the capitals and numbers probably originated with me but with no heinous intention at all.'

The entire court, the party floor, and every single character on the page were completely transfixed by this tale of woe from the number 1. So it was all down to a number who thought he was a letter. Red brought the proceedings to an end and harrumphed himself to a summation of the trial.

'Well, my new found friends, and while we're at it, my old lost friends, and let us not forget, my yet to meet friends, and as we have forgotten, my long forgotten friends, and last but not least, lest we do forget, my absent friends.'

Red brought the hammer down on the bench with some force, in a dynamic version of a punctuation mark. Red was the master of ceremonies now. During his speech the hammer would come down with some regularity and on the floor, the commas, the full stops, the colons and the semi-colons would argue which strike represented them, and they invented a game whereby the punctuation marks with the highest score of hammer blows would win, for they could not resist the pull of punctuation. An exclamation mark came over and insisted that she too be allowed to play which was immediately permitted. Oh good she said, this really is a punctuation party! Strike one!

'Has the jury reached a verdict?'

'We have.'

'What is your verdict?'

'Guilty.'

There was a hubbub of turmoil amongst the capitals and numbers now, which became even more so, if not terrified, when Red put on a black cap. The numbers began to count down in panic; the capitals took to stretching their necks and checking that they were still there. By the time Red began to speak again everything in the dock, capitals and numbers both, and nearly everything on the floor too, were italicized in their eagerness to know what came next, some with trepidation, some with terror, some with insouciance, and some with intent to whoop no matter what.

'I hope you like my hat, goes rather well with the old red font eh? The Black Hat and the Red Font, now there's a title, if not a tittle, my, my, my, but this has been a tale of woe, adventure, horror, hope, loss, despair, and insistent humour to boot. Well, just what are we going to do about you lot? You've been found guilty, but you've been kind of absolved, you've been behaving with a selfishness that betrays the malign effect of the capital I. Yes, the singular pronoun. Straight up; straight down; vertical. I was in serious danger of taking over from the hyphen by this point, though it's doubtful whether any letter or word would take this hyphen's arms. So, the other capitals will be free to go, but you will share Is' sentence, you numbers will tarry a while, but you will also be released, but not until you hear me out, and not until I decide what to do with this singularly selfish singular pronoun.'

All the other capitals and all the numbers began to make even more space around I than was normal, the capital I being of a nature that kept more space around him than any other letter, but this new space around him made this singular pronoun singularly singular, to say the least, or should that be most, given the situation. Mind you, his current pro-hyphen stance demanded a more substantial space than normal anyway.

'You were always the subject of the sentence you were in weren't you? So you thought yourself above everybody else, but unfortunately that egotistical attitude was not reciprocated by any of the others, so you had to be better than them. Why do I need those words? Well, try IIIIIIIIIIIIIIIIIIIIIII for size and see if you can work it out? It was worse than that though because you even resented the space around you because that wasn't you, but again you never thought it through did you?

'There's your vociferous agreement system for you, that's **IIIIIII** without the space, which is all you, all you, anything beyond you was, well, just beyond you. That completely black line was your aim, oh you never thought so, Hell no, but that's what you were after. The information at the end is the same as at the start, no progress, no story, no tangents, no digression, and no change at all, just you and only you.'

Red's hammer was coming down and the punctuation competition was coming on splendidly, with what was looking like a straight fight off between the commas and the exclamation mark, though the commas were suspecting a bit of cheating from their shrieking competitor.

'You were death to meaning, death to sentences, death to words, and death to letters, punctuation marks and any other entity that wasn't you. It's no wonder you promoted acronyms and abbreviations, you are an abbreviation, you're used when we can't be bothered using our names, so you thought you'd just abbreviate everything to death and you'd acronym space out of existence. You know, letters and words are just scribbles on space, nothing else, and without that space we can't leave our narrative trail, and we can't tell our stories without it, and neither can you, but sadly you don't actually have a story at all, for you are truly just a stand in for the unknown person. You thought that if there was no space there would only be you, but there would in fact be nothing, nothing at all.'

It was neck and neck between the exclamation marks and the commas.

'In your insane quest for oblivion, you should really have a chat with the fates you know, you gave the numbers carte blanche to count any way they liked, then you just reduced everything to numbers, but you could never cover everything with those numbers, so you'd do it again, but each time you did it, you created more and more beyond the numbers, until you realised this so then you just counted and counted up and up and up, never knowing where you started. You used acronyms that stood for utterly opaque terms which meant they started with no real starting point, nothing was based on anything. What a mess. You know the capital letter A stands for the indefinite article, to get to a definite article you need the word 'the', now the difference is this, you can't define things by a single letter, you need at least a word, you need at least three letters in combination, anything less doesn't work.'

The commas had won.

'I sentence the numbers to count downwards for the rest of this tale. I sentence the capitals other than the personal pronoun to provide carriage to any ghosts left in this story for the remainder of this story. I sentence the personal pronoun to flatness for the remainder of this tale. That is my judgment. This court is now closed.

The full stop finished the game.

The punctuation party was swinging away nicely now, Red, the commas, '*u*', Zero and Stopper all met up, to end the tale.

'Hey Stopper,' said '*u*', 'how much of that number 1's story was true?'

'About two thirds, at a guess.'

'So it was a stretch?'

'Of course, but sometimes you need to stretch.'

'So what about the numbers, Stopper?'

'The numbers are of no consequence until someone uses them, '*u*', but you know in a way that's the same for us, but the difference is this; it doesn't matter how eloquent, how poetic a writer you are, you cannot ever capture all of what you want to say, you can only show the way. You see language is other referent, so it's always pointing out others, always trying to reach out beyond its' limits. Numbers are always self referent, they only ever talk about themselves, that's why they are so aloof, they care not a whit for the referent imposed on them and the capitals never really understood that. Reducing things to numbers really does reduce things, it leaves too much out, ignores the innumerable, and that's too big to ignore. Language doesn't ignore it, it doesn't reach it, but then it never claims to, but it does point the way, it's expansive, and that's how it should be, an ever opening flower of nectar, nutrition, and the wisdom to know that counting crows don't fly.'

The group of them wandered off back into one of the later paragraphs chatting and laughing their way back into the story, and as they strolled their way towards the end, and each of them, one by one, dropped off, they thought they saw a ghost flit in another line, and they thought they heard a whisper of Stop-it, but like a will of the wisp, like a not quite caught memory, they shimmered and faded before they could last. At last there were only Stopper and Zero left, and they wandered on talking and loving and hoping and waiting until the story starts again, as they reawake in another subconscious, and tell their tale again.